Language Teacher Education and Technology

Advances in Digital Language Learning and Teaching

Series Editors: Michael Thomas, University of Central Lancashire, UK, Mark Peterson, Kyoto University, Japan, and Mark Warschauer, University of California – Irvine, USA

Today's language educators need support to understand how their learners are changing and the ways technology can be used to aid their teaching and learning strategies. The movement toward different modes of language learning – from presence-based to autonomous as well as blended and fully online modes – requires different skill sets such as e-moderation and new ways of designing and developing language learning tasks in the digital age. Theoretical studies that include practical case studies and high quality empirical studies incorporating critical perspectives are necessary to move the field further. This new series is committed to providing such an outlet for high quality work on digital language learning and teaching. Volumes in the series will focus on a number of areas including but not limited to:

- task-based learning and teaching approaches utilizing technology
- language-learner creativity
- e-moderation and teaching languages online
- blended language learning
- designing courses for online and distance language learning
- mobile-assisted language learning
- autonomous language learning, both in and outside of formal educational contexts
- the use of web 2.0/social media technologies
- immersive and virtual language-learning environments
- digital game-based language learning
- language educator professional development with digital technologies
- teaching language skills with technologies

Enquiries about the series can be made by contacting the series editors: Michael Thomas (MThomas4@uclan.acuk), Mark Peterson (tufsmp@yahoo.com) and Mark Warschauer (markw@uci.edu).

Titles in the Series

Autonomy and Foreign Language Learning in a Virtual Learning Environment, Miranda Hamilton

Online Teaching and Learning: Sociocultural Perspectives, edited by Carla Meskill

Task-Based Language Learning in a Real-World Digital Environment, edited by Paul Seedhouse

Teaching Languages with Technology: Communicative Approaches to Interactive Whiteboard Use, edited by Euline Cutrim Schmid and Shona Whyte

WorldCALL, edited by Ana Gimeno, Mike Levy, Françoise Blin and David Barr

Language Teacher Education and Technology

Approaches and Practices

Edited by
Jeong-Bae Son and Scott Windeatt

Bloomsbury Academic
An imprint of Bloomsbury Publishing Plc

B L O O M S B U R Y
LONDON • OXFORD • NEW YORK • NEW DELHI • SYDNEY

Bloomsbury Academic
An imprint of Bloomsbury Publishing Plc

50 Bedford Square
London
WC1B 3DP
UK

1385 Broadway
New York
NY 10018
USA

www.bloomsbury.com

BLOOMSBURY and the Diana logo are trademarks of Bloomsbury Publishing Plc

First published 2017

British Library Cataloguing-in-Publication Data
A catalogue record for this book is available from the British Library.

ISBN: HB: 978-1-3500-2040-5
ePDF: 978-1-3500-2041-2
ePub: 978-1-3500-2042-9

Library of Congress Cataloguing-in-Publication Data
Names: Son, Jeong-Bae, editor. | Windeatt, Scott, editor.
Title: Language teacher education and technology : approaches and practices / edited by Jeong-Bae Son and Scott Windeatt.
Description: London ; New York : Bloomsbury Academic, [2017] |
Series: Advances in digital language learning and teaching |
Includes bibliographical references and index.
Identifiers: LCCN 2016058376| ISBN 9781350020405 (hb) |
ISBN 9781350020429 (epub)
Subjects: LCSH: Language and languages–Study and teaching–Computer network resources. | Language and languages–Computer-assisted instruction. |
Language transfer (Language learning)–Technological innovations. |
Internet in education. | Educational technology.
Classification: LCC P53.285 .L34 2017 | DDC 418.0078/5–dc23
LC record available at https://lccn.loc.gov/2016058376

Cover design by James Watson
Cover image © Shutterstock

Series: Advances in Digital Language Learning and Teaching

Typeset by Newgen Knowledge Works Pvt Ltd., Chennai, India.

Contents

Illustrations

Tables

Figures

Notes on Contributors

Christine Bauer-Ramazani, instructor at Saint Michael's College, teaches in the intensive English, the academic English, as well as the MATESOL programme. Her main field of research and professional engagement have been the design and teaching of online/distance courses, exemplified by her co-founding of the Electronic Village Online (EVO) of TESOL (2000), her design and teaching of online courses for TESOL (Teaching Writing Online, Teaching Reading and Writing, and Online Learning for Campus-based Teaching) as well as her Computer-Assisted Language Learning (CALL) course (online since 2000) and Curriculum and Syllabus Design Online (online since 2012). Christine has authored book chapters and articles, and practices the integration of technology in her courses. She has given plenaries on the topic in several countries and regularly presents in the CALL-IS sessions at TESOL. Her articles and presentations focus on project-based and flipped learning in blended and online courses.

Paul Gruba is a Senior Lecturer in Applied Linguistics, University of Melbourne. Starting as a Peace Corps volunteer in the early 1980s, Paul has built a career on teaching English in Australia, Mali, Japan and the United States. He earned a PhD in the late 1990s through an investigation of the role of digital video media in second language listening comprehension. He has published widely on research to do with listening theory, assessment and new media, and, most recently, blended language programme evaluation. Paul's current research continues to focus on multimodal second language listening and language programme evaluation.

Philip Hubbard, PhD, is Senior Lecturer in Linguistics and Director of English for Foreign Students at the Stanford University Language Center. For the past three decades, he has devoted his professional career to developing the field of CALL. He has published widely on CALL listening, learner training, theory, research and methodology. In terms of teacher training, he has a widely cited article on CALL and the future of teacher education (*CALICO Journal*, 2008), was co-editor of and contributor to *Teacher Education in CALL*, 2006, and served on the task force that created the TESOL Technology Standards (TESOL, 2008).

The content in the support website for his Foundations of CALL course is freely available at http://web.stanford.edu/~efs/callcourse2/.

Greg Kessler is the Director of the Language Resource Center and Associate Professor of CALL in the Department of Linguistics at Ohio University. He is also an affiliated faculty member in Instructional Technology in the Patton College of Education. His research addresses instructional technology, teacher preparation, language teaching and associated human behaviour. He has published in *Language Learning & Technology*, *Computer-Assisted Language Learning*, and *CALICO Journal*. He has also written a number of books and book chapters, including the *TESOL Technology Standards*. He is currently the editor of the *Advances in CALL Research & Practice* CALICO Book Series.

Mike Levy is Honorary Professor of Second Language Studies in the School of Languages and Cultures at the University of Queensland. His main field of research investigates the ways in which the attributes of new technologies, especially mobile technologies, work to mediate interactions when students are learning another language. He is also particularly interested in teacher education and qualitative approaches to research design in CALL. He is the co-author of *CALL Dimensions: Options and Issues in CALL* (2006).

Paul J. Moore is a Lecturer in the School of Languages and Cultures at the University of Queensland, where he teaches courses in applied linguistics, intercultural communication and language and technology. His research interests include second language learning and social/cognitive perspectives on task-based interaction.

Eddy Moran has a PhD in CALL from the University of Newcastle and has been teaching CALL, Language Assessment and SLA Theory and Research at the University of Stirling since 2005. He teaches three CALL modules focusing on use of existing web-based resources, multimedia authoring and blended delivery technologies. His current research interests in CALL are blended delivery in teacher training and use of the flipped approach in EFL teaching. Apart from CALL research, he is a member of a British Council–funded research team investigating postgraduate students' expectations for masters' level TESOL programmes in the United Kingdom. His most recent publications and presentations have focused on student perceptions of the use of video tutorials in EFL teacher training and the application of video tutorial materials in distance team teaching.

Gary Motteram is a Senior Lecturer in Education at the University of Manchester, United Kingdom. He set up the first ever Master's that linked educational technology and TESOL, which was also the first online degree of its type. He has presented at conferences and published regularly in the fields of technology in language learning and technology-supported teacher education. His most recent book is *Innovations in Learning Technologies for ELT*. He has managed a number of international projects for the University of Manchester, including eChinaUK and AVALON (avalonlearning.eu), and he ran a two-year research project exploring what teachers do with technology. He was a member of the European Union–funded Euroversity (euroversity.eu) network and has most recently managed an evaluation of the ReflectED project (https://educationendowmentfoundation.org.uk/evaluation/projects/reflected-meta-cognition) for the Education Endowment Foundation.

Denise E. Murray is Professor Emeritus at Macquarie University in Sydney and at San José State University in California. She has a long history as a language teacher educator, having been the Executive Director of the Adult Migrant English Program Research Centre and of the National Centre for English Language Teaching and Research at Macquarie University from 2000 to 2006. Prior to her appointment at Macquarie, she was founding Chair of the Department of Linguistics and Language Development at San José State University. For seven years, she served on the Board of Directors of TESOL International, including a term as President in 1996–1997. Her research interests include computer-assisted language learning; cross-cultural literacy; the use of the learners' L1 in the second language classroom; the intersection of language, society and technology; settlement of adult immigrants; OLTE; language education policy; and leadership in language education. She has published her work in seventeen books and more than 100 articles.

Jeong-Bae Son, PhD, is an Associate Professor in Applied Linguistics and TESOL at the University of Southern Queensland, Australia. His areas of specialization are computer-assisted language learning and language teacher education. He has developed a number of CALL applications, published extensively in the field of CALL and conducted seminars and workshops on CALL around the world. His edited books include *Computer-Assisted Language Learning: Concepts, Contexts and Practices* (2004), *Internet-Based Language Learning: Pedagogies and Technologies* (2009) and *Computer-Assisted Language Learning: Learners, Teachers and Tools* (2014). He is currently the President of the Asia-Pacific Association for Computer-Assisted Language Learning (APACALL), Co-Chair of the Globalization and Localization in Computer-Assisted Language Learning (GLoCALL) Conference, Director of Technology-Enhanced Language Learning Research Network (TELLRN) and Editor of the APACALL Book Series.

Scott Windeatt has taught and lectured in many countries and is currently Senior Lecturer in Applied Linguistics and TESOL in the School of Education Communication and Language Sciences at Newcastle University in the UK, where he has worked for the last twenty-five years. He supervises PhD students and teaches on the MA in Applied Linguistics and TESOL, offering modules on Computer-Assisted Language Learning and e-Learning for Languages, and contributes to the Research Methods module. His main research interests are computer-assisted language learning, e-learning and teacher-training. His publications include *The Internet: A Resource Book for Teachers*, with David Hardisty and David Eastment; *The Impact of Computer-Based Feedback on Students' Written Work*, with Khaled El-Ebyary; *Low-Achieving Language Learners in Self-Directed Multimedia Environments: Transforming Understanding*, with Pei-Lun Kao; and *How Language Teachers Become Effective Users of CALL for Online Teaching and Learning: A Case Study of Their Developmental Processes in a Transformative E-Training Course*, with Sandra Morales-Rios.

Preface

Computers are now part of everyday life and are as likely to be found in the pocket or a bag as in the computer room. Familiarity with a technology, however, does not necessarily translate into an understanding of how it can be used for learning and teaching. Computer technology plays an increasingly important role in language learning and in courses for language teachers. While courses that include an element of training in the use of technology are now delivered by a range of institutions, such training generally originated in universities and on postgraduate courses mainly because they were the institutions that had the resources when computer technology was expensive and beyond the reach of many institutions. Given the extraordinary developments in technology since the inception of these courses – from mainframe-based systems to the seemingly ubiquitous availability of smartphones, tablets and access to the Internet – and the advent of a population of so-called digital generations, courses for training teachers in the use of technology for language learning can be seen as having arrived at a crossroads. Is it necessary to train teachers in the use of technology, or is it sufficient for them to develop an understanding of second language acquisition processes and classroom methodology? For that reason, now seems to be an ideal time to examine these courses and to tap into the experience of those who have developed and taught them. The insights gained from such an examination will help the reader understand how and why such courses have been designed and are delivered in the way they are, how their design and delivery have evolved over the years, and what direction the courses might take in the future.

The inspiration for this book was a symposium organized by Jeong-Bae Son at the AILA World Congress 2014 in Brisbane, Australia, which brought together computer-assisted language learning (CALL) teacher educators from Australia, the United Kingdom and the United States who had considerable experience in running CALL training courses. The aim of the symposium was to identify common themes and differences in the courses they offered and to discuss the challenges they faced and future directions. From the symposium, we could see a need to investigate the current status of formal CALL courses offered for language teachers in a wider way and understand what and how other CALL teacher educators actually do in terms of theoretical approaches to the teaching of their courses and practical components of the courses they consider in their contexts.

For language teachers, training – both in- and pre-service – is increasingly taking place as part of a course leading to a postgraduate degree. This book represents the first overview of a topic that is relevant to most postgraduate courses in Applied Linguistics or TESOL across the globe. The use of technology for language learning and teaching is increasingly common but, as is so often the case, training for teachers in how to use the technology remains limited to a large extent by a lack of expertise among trainers. The discussion of approaches to training teachers in the use of technology (specifically CALL) adopted in areas of Australia, the United Kingdom and the United States, where such training has been available for a relatively long time and is arguably the most developed, will provide valuable information for those already involved in this field and inspiration for those who have some interest in carrying out this kind of training but as yet have little or no experience.

The authors in this book are well placed to offer insights into how teachers can be taught to use CALL, how CALL training courses can be adapted as technology evolves and how teachers can be helped to adapt to such changes beyond the courses. They were given a wide brief, which was to choose an introductory CALL training course they are responsible for, to describe the course and its context, to highlight any features of the course or issues that they wanted to draw to the readers' attention and to discuss how they felt the course was likely to evolve.

Overall, this book provides a unique opportunity to gain insights into language teacher education from the perspectives of CALL teacher educators. As editors, we are grateful to all authors and reviewers who were involved in the publication of the book. We appreciate their collaboration, cooperation, patience and willingness to work with us.

Jeong-Bae Son
Scott Windeatt

1

Teacher Training in Computer-Assisted Language Learning

Voices of Teacher Educators

Jeong-Bae Son
University of Southern Queensland, Australia
and
Scott Windeatt
Newcastle University, UK

Introduction

A variety of technologies have been used in education over the centuries. Since the advent of the personal computer, those technologies have converged so that, in many cases, technology in education in general and language teaching in particular has now come to be seen as synonymous with the use of computers in various manifestations. Professional training for teachers in computer-assisted language learning (CALL) has evolved in that time in parallel with ideas about language learning, changes in approaches to teacher education and developments in technology. Through CALL training courses, pre-service and in-service language teachers are guided and encouraged to use computer technology in meaningful and practical ways.

Language teachers' competence in CALL is a crucial factor affecting the implementation of CALL (e.g., Hubbard, 2008; Kessler, 2006; Son, 2004, 2014). It is therefore of concern that many language teachers are not adequately prepared to make effective use of CALL or to confidently identify and evaluate potential CALL solutions. This can be due to many different factors. Teachers often indicate that they do not have sufficient opportunity to attend CALL training courses and the CALL training they receive is not appropriate to their needs.

They also point out that, once they enter the teaching profession, there is a lack of support for the skills they have acquired. These realities raise the question of how teachers can be effectively trained and helped to develop their knowledge and skills for the use of technology in language teaching. What existing pedagogical and technical knowledge and skills can be transferred when using technology for language teaching, and how can such a transfer be facilitated? What new knowledge and skills need to be developed? What roles should theory and practice play in a course? To what extent should the mode of delivery of a course match the way in which the teachers might use the technology? How can we help teachers acquire the underlying skills and attitudes which will encourage them to develop a critical understanding of the potential offered by new developments in technology?

This book describes and discusses CALL training courses that are currently offered in postgraduate programmes in the English-speaking world and looks into how those courses have evolved to take account of changes in technology and in ideas about language learning and teaching. All of the courses represent experience gained in providing CALL training over a period of at least a decade, but some have their origins in training initially developed three decades ago, when personal computers first began to appear in educational institutions in any numbers.

In this first chapter, we explore trends, issues, developments and challenges in CALL teacher education in relation to nine CALL training courses presented in nine chapters (Chapter 2 to Chapter 10) of this book (see Appendix A for an overview of the courses). In order to provide an in-depth picture of how the courses provide different solutions to what, on the surface, should be the same problem, we identify the variety of approaches the different courses take to the choice of methodology, course content, course delivery and course evaluation.

CALL training courses

Course titles

Reflecting developments in technology and its use, a wide variety of terms and acronyms have been used over the years to refer to the use of computer technology for learning. Computer-Assisted Learning (CAL) and Computer-Based Learning (CBL) refer to the use of computers in general education while

Information and Communication Technology (ICT) emphasizes the use of technology as a means not only of disseminating information, but also of communicating and interacting with other users. In language learning, terms such as Network-Based Language Learning (NBLL), Web-Based Language Learning (WBLL) and Mobile-Assisted Language Learning (MALL) have been coined to describe a focus on specific forms of technology, while the increasing range of computer-based technologies available to learners and teachers is reflected in other broader terms such as Technology-Enhanced Language Learning (TELL), e-learning and digital learning. Nevertheless, the term CALL continues to be widely used, and it can be argued that CALL, rather like applied linguistics, is an overarching term encompassing an ever-growing range of applications. The courses described in this book reflect this view with titles that are mostly variations on the term CALL. All are introductory courses; some of the institutions also offer other CALL-related courses focusing on more specialized aspects of the use of computers for language learning and teaching.

Target audience

The scope of this book is deliberately limited to covering CALL training courses offered in Master's degree programmes. Thus, the courses all form part of Master's degree programmes and the course participants are likely to be postgraduates although one course (Chapter 10), as a mini-course, is open to undergraduates as well as postgraduates and its resources are freely available on the web for anyone to use without having to register for the degree. While students in the CALL courses are more likely to be experienced teachers, most of these degree programmes cater for students both with and without teaching experience. The fact that the courses are aimed at students from a wide range of different countries, with varied levels of teaching experience, in programmes with either a more general or a more specialized applied linguistics focus has resulted in varied solutions to the problem of how best to provide CALL training at the Master's level.

Mode of delivery

While all but one of those courses described in this book are offered face-to-face on-campus, there is a growing trend towards online or blended delivery of CALL courses. One course is only offered online (Chapter 9), whereas four of the others have both on-campus and online versions (Chapters 3, 4, 5 and 8).

Three of the chapters deal with some of the main issues that face those involved in offering online courses. Chapter 9 in particular provides a detailed discussion of the design and management of one such online CALL course, and of the challenges this mode of delivery poses, including the wide geographical spread of course participants, and the consequent need to manage interaction across time-zones – an issue which is also discussed in Chapter 5. Such problems are common to all online courses, but for courses in training teachers to use CALL, there is a specific problem posed by the need to provide hands-on practice with hardware and software which may not be easily available in the context in which an individual is studying, or may be difficult to provide for them online (Chapter 4).

Course objectives

Any course for training teachers to teach language is predicated on the assumption that participants understand central concepts of second language acquisition (SLA), and the main aim of the courses described in this book is to explore approaches to harnessing technology in order to enhance SLA. The most common objectives are for students to learn how to locate language learning resources and materials (Chapters 2, 6, 7 and 8), evaluate them (Chapters 2, 4, 5, 6, 7, 8 and 9) and understand more generally the potential uses and limitations of CALL (Chapters 6 and 7). Most courses have the acquisition of skills in using CALL materials and resources with learners as one of their stated objectives (Chapters 2, 4, 6, 7, 8 and 9), and one course refers specifically to an understanding of teacher roles in CALL (Chapter 4). Creating materials is a stated objective for four of the courses (Chapters 2, 7, 8 and 9), and two refer specifically to learning how to use a learning management system (LMS) (Chapters 8 and 9). An understanding of research in CALL may be inferred from the reference to work on literature on CALL in most of the courses, but three refer to this as a specific objective (Chapters 4, 5 and 9).

Location within a degree programme

CALL courses in a Master's degree are generally intended to help students transfer their experience of language teaching to the use of technology with language learners, and to explore the application of ideas about language learning and teaching encountered elsewhere in the degree. For students with little or no teaching experience, the prerequisite or co-requisite courses will determine what the course instructor can expect the students to bring to the CALL course. Three courses (Chapters 5, 6 and 8) are compulsory in specific degree programmes and are linked either to other applied linguistics courses as co-requisites (i.e., students are required to take those courses alongside the CALL course) or to a range of other CALL courses that can be taken in parallel or later in the degree. Those courses that are campus-based are all delivered within one semester, although even here there is variation, as the length of a semester varies between eleven and fifteen weeks, with one course (Chapter 10) running for only eight weeks. Weekly contact hours vary between two and four hours, supplemented by a total of up to around 180 hours for independent study.

Views of learning

CALL courses are likely to reflect current mainstream views of SLA and therefore incorporate at least some elements of constructivism or social constructivist approaches, especially in relation to topics on computer-mediated communication (CMC). While the courses described in this book generally adopt a social-constructivist approach (e.g., Beck & Kosnik, 2006; Williams & Burden, 1997), in practice, the approach is realized in a number of different ways, including a loop-input approach (Woodward, 2003), experiential learning (Kolb, 1984), problem solving (Newell & Simon, 1972), communities of practice (Lave & Wenger, 1991), communities of inquiry (Garrison, Anderson, & Archer, 2000) and transformative learning theory (Mezirow, 2000). Some courses specifically refer to constructivism or social constructivist principles as the basis for, or an important element in, the design of their courses (Chapters 3, 7, 8 and 9), and a detailed discussion is provided of how those principles are translated into practice during the course (Chapter 8). It is also likely that exploring the use of CMC and social networks (Chapters 2, 3, 4, 5, 8, 9 and 10) may not only reflect, but also encourage an interactionist view of SLA.

Teaching techniques

The most widely referenced teaching technique involves selected readings (Chapters 2, 3, 4, 5, 6, 7, 8 and 9) generally linked to group discussions (Chapters 2, 3, 4, 8 and 9) and tasks linked to their own teaching situations (Chapter 4). Reference is made to lectures or demonstrations (Chapters 2 and 8) although all courses presumably make use of one or both of those techniques; student tasks and presentations (Chapter 10); and peer support or collaborative tasks (Chapter 9).

Course contents

There has been little work until relatively recently on the specification of the skills and knowledge language teachers need in order to teach effectively with technology. Hampel and Stickler (2005) and Salmon (2011) provide suggested models for the skills and knowledge needed for online language teaching. Hubbard and Levy (2006) have identified technical and pedagogical skills and knowledge they feel language teachers should possess in order to teach with computers. Also, Healey et al. (2011) have compiled a comprehensive list of skills and knowledge (standards) that teachers should acquire at increasingly advanced stages of competence in using computers for language teaching. An important feature in some of the courses presented in this book is the adoption of TESOL Technology Standards Framework (TESOL, 2008), which helps instructors and course designers make decisions about the contents of CALL courses and how progression through different levels of skills and knowledge can be managed (Chapters 3, 9 and 10).

The courses vary in scope and in the emphasis placed on different topics, but there are a number of features that most have in common. Most courses begin with some historical perspective (Chapters 2, 3, 4, 6, 8, 9 and 10) and move on to an evaluation of existing software or language teaching resources (Chapters 2, 4, 6, 7, 8, 9 and 10). Some use materials creation as a way of understanding how ideas about language learning can be translated into CALL materials (Chapters 6 and 7). Most refer specifically to the teaching of language skills (Chapters 2, 3, 6, 7, 9 and 10). Some refer specifically to the use of non-language specific software, including CMC (Chapters 2, 5, 6, 9 and 10) and social networks (Chapter 8). Other topics, which are referred to in some of the course descriptions, include virtual worlds (Chapters 5 and 10), gaming (Chapters 5, 9 and 10), mobile learning (Chapters 2, 3, 9 and 10) and managing CALL resources (Chapter 4). All courses involve a mixture of theory and practice, and one refers specifically to consideration of SLA topics (Chapter 3). Given the speed of technological developments, there are a number of topics which are likely to be given greater prominence, or added, in the future (see the Developments section of this chapter).

Assessment

Each CALL course provides details of how students are assessed. Assessment practices vary in terms of the number and nature of assessment tasks, linked as they are to the objectives of the course and influenced by the underlying design principles and course philosophy. There is some discussion of needs analysis and formative assessment (Chapters 2 and 9), but for summative assessment, all courses require the students to write at least one academic paper in some form, such as a literature review. A number of courses include at least one assessment task involving CALL materials evaluation (Chapters 2, 4, 6, 9 and 10). Some involve the creation of computer-based materials, together with a discussion of considerations in designing the materials (Chapters 2, 7 and 8). Other forms of assessment involve lesson planning (Chapters 4 and 5) and a takeaway test (Chapter 6). There is also a discussion of how students themselves participate in the design and construction of aspects of the course, including student assessment (Chapter 9), and one course evaluates students by means of an exam which is constructed collaboratively by both the teacher and the students (Chapter 8).

Course evaluation

One of the great difficulties with any course is knowing not only what the immediate benefits might be for participants, but also how the skills and knowledge acquired in the course might benefit the participants in the longer term. This is especially relevant to training in the use of technology, which is in a permanent state of change. A course in technology for language learning has to involve an understanding of underlying concepts and strategies for adapting to change. End-of-course evaluation by students is valuable in helping determine how a course can be improved, and can be used to validate particular aspects of the course. Bearing in mind that a Master's degree is intended to have a long-term effect on the graduates, additionally, delayed post-course evaluation, difficult though it may be to carry out, can provide useful insights into the extent to which the longer-term objectives of a course have been achieved (Chapter 7).

Developments

All of the courses described in this book are well-established, and some have been offered in one form or another for over fifteen, twenty-five or thirty years (Chapters 2, 4, 5, 7 and 10). For many the approach and methodology adopted has remained fundamentally the same, or, despite changes, is clearly linked to that adopted in earlier versions of the course (Chapters 2, 4, 5 and 9). Developments that have taken place are connected to changes in the field of applied linguistics as a whole (Chapter 2) and are inevitably shaped by developments in technology and changes in the nature of the student intake.

The main technological impetus for change has come from the wide use of the Internet, the availability of mobile technologies, including wearable technology (Chapter 5) and the transition from analogue to digital technologies (Chapter 7). Web 2.0 technologies, including social networks (Chapters 8, 9 and 10), and more specific applications such as games (Chapters 2 and 5) and virtual worlds (Chapters 2 and 3) also figure in these courses. In addition, reference is made to the value of low-tech CALL through the use of basic mobile phones in certain contexts (Chapter 5), and to the potential for collaboration among teachers and teacher trainers through the use of open educational resources (Chapter 4). In the future, developments in artificial intelligence (AI) may well have the most profound effect on CALL, including applications based on AI such as speech recognition and machine translation (Chapter 2).

Apart from technological developments, there have also been changes in the nature of the student intake. Courses originally designed for students who were new to technology have been increasingly adapted to allow for the growing familiarity with technology of generations such as 'digital natives' (Prensky, 2001). As a result, courses move away from a technology driven approach towards one that is more language learning driven (Chapter 5). At the same time, there may be unexpected gaps in the students' understanding of the potential of general office applications such as certain features of word processing and spreadsheet software (Chapters 5 and 7). In addition, while Applied Linguistics Master's courses were, for the most part, originally intended for students with teaching experience, there is a growing trend towards admission of students with little or no teaching experience (Chapters 3, 6, 7 and 9) – this will affect not only the objectives and contents of the course, but also decisions on how the course is located within the degree programme.

Challenges

Technology-based training courses present particular challenges to those designing and delivering them. Ensuring that appropriate up-to-date hardware and software is available is an issue, and the need for, and reliance on, reliable infrastructure and the availability of helpful technical assistance are central to the provision of technology-based courses. This is exacerbated by the rate of changes in the technology, requiring constant updating not only of hardware and software, but of skills and training materials as well (Chapters 5 and 9). Such changes affect not only the technology itself, but also published research on the use of technology. One feature of the pace of developments is that textbooks in CALL are quickly outdated; hence the emphasis in most courses on journal articles and online resources which can be quickly updated, but which also require teachers and course designers to ensure that they keep track of relevant studies.

Additional challenges arise in technology-based courses that are delivered online, including scheduling difficulties when working across time zones (Chapter 5 and 9) and changes in the LMS that forms the hub for online courses, which can cause difficulties for students, and impose a significant increase in the workload on instructors (Chapter 9), with no guarantee of compensation for the additional time commitment required. Where both on-campus and online versions of a courses are offered, there are also issues of equality of opportunity as it can be difficult to provide equivalent hands-on practice with hardware and software for students studying in the two different modes (Chapter 4).

Adapting courses to meet the needs of participants in any particular cohort is an important aspect of any course, but may be a particular issue for CALL as both knowledge of applied linguistics and experience of teaching have to be taken into account, as well as levels of familiarity with technology. Needs analysis and formative assessment are important techniques that provide a more immediate means of identifying the requirements of a particular group of students, but equally important is the need for students to develop self-training and collaboration strategies (Chapter 4), not only for online course participants, but also for on-campus students. This is important partly because, as technology develops at an ever-increasing pace, students will have to find ways of updating their own skills and knowledge once the course has finished, and because CALL courses, especially introductory courses of the kind described here, can only cover a relatively small proportion of what is an increasingly broad subject (Chapters 2 and 10). The development of such strategies is similarly important in helping participants develop and maintain motivation for what can be quite demanding courses.

The issue of the limited coverage which these courses can provide is highlighted by the lack of a core curriculum in a subject which is still 'young and dynamic' (Chapter 10), and a distinction is drawn between 'depth-first' or 'breadth-first' courses (Chapter 10), suggesting that any one course can either deal with a limited range of topics in greater detail or with a broad range of topics in less detail.

Whichever approach is adopted, within any one course, decisions still have to be made about the relative proportion of time that can be spent on, for example, theory or practice (Chapter 6), and about the nature and coverage of course assessments (Chapter 4). This is a challenge which can be met, to some extent at least, by providing a suite of CALL courses, each of which offers a more specialized focus (Chapters 5, 6 and 8), although for many institutions, including the majority of those represented in this book, no more than one or two CALL courses are on offer.

The book

This book provides a unique opportunity to hear the inside stories of nine CALL courses offered at nine different universities in Australia, the United Kingdom and the United States. From Chapter 2 to Chapter 10, the courses are described and discussed by CALL teacher educators who teach the courses. Each chapter consists of the following sections: Introduction; Context; Course Description; Features and Issues; and Future Directions. Specifically, Mike Levy and Paul J. Moore in Chapter 2 present their course titled 'Language and Technology'. They describe the history, role and content of the course with a general discussion on the ever-changing field of CALL. In Chapter 3, Paul Gruba presents his course titled 'Technology and Language Learning'. He describes the course syllabus with three themes: key trends; skills and technologies; and research and evaluation. In Chapter 4, Jeong-Bae Son presents his course titled 'Computer-Assisted Language Learning'. He discusses the modular approach taken by the course, which has three main modules: background; research; and language teachers in CALL environments. In Chapter 5, Gary Motteram presents his course titled 'Language Learning and Technology'. He describes various topics covered by the course and explores the impact of developments in mobile technologies on the course. In Chapter 6, Eddy Moran presents his course titled 'Introduction to CALL'. He discusses the underlying approach taken in the course and the content of the course, which covers what teachers need to know to be competent in the use of online resources. In Chapter 7, Scott Windeatt presents his course titled 'Computer-Assisted Language Learning'. He discusses the evolution of the course and the long-term effect of doing the course with the results of post-course evaluation. In Chapter 8, Greg Kessler presents his course titled 'Computers in Language Teaching', which is a single component of a series of five CALL courses offered at his linguistics department. He discusses how and why theory and practice are balanced in the course. In Chapter 9, Christine Bauer-Ramazani presents her course titled 'Computer-Assisted Language Learning Online'. She discusses the pedagogical principles and components of the course in alignment with the TESOL Technology Standards Framework (TESOL, 2008). In Chapter 10, Philip Hubbard presents his course titled 'CALL Mini-Course' that is offered as a complement to an ESL/EFL methodology class. He describes the content of the course (8 units) and discusses how the course is related to the TESOL Technology Standards Framework (TESOL, 2008). Finally, Denise Murray in Chapter 11 looks at CALL teacher education in terms of content and processes linked to the chapters in this book and emphasizes the need for formal CALL coursework, institutional support and ongoing professional development.

Conclusion

CALL teacher training is primarily offered in the form of postgraduate courses at universities. What the courses offer and how they are delivered depend on a number of factors, including course objectives, course contents, teaching techniques and teaching contexts. The chapters in this book explore ways of developing language teachers' knowledge and skills for using CALL and discuss the factors affecting CALL teacher education in general and formal CALL courses in particular. They offer theoretical and practical aspects of CALL courses offered at universities and elaborate issues and challenges the authors of the chapters (CALL teacher educators) deal with. It is hoped that the insights this book provides into language teacher education for CALL will be of practical help to teachers and to those responsible for training teachers to teach in digital learning environments.

References

Beck, C., & Kosnik, C. (2006). *Innovations in teacher education: A social constructivist approach*. Albany, NY: State University of New York Press.

Garrison, R. D., Anderson, T., & Archer, W. (2000). Critical inquiry in a text-based environment: Computer conferencing in higher education. *Internet and Higher Education*, 2(2–3), 87–105.

Hampel, R., & Stickler, U. (2005). New skills for new classrooms: Training tutors to teach languages online. *Computer Assisted Language Learning*, *18*(4), 311–326.

Healey, D., Hanson-Smith, E., Hubbard, P., Ioannou-Georgiou, S., Kessler, G., & Ware, P. (2011). *TESOL Technology standards: Description, implementation, integration*. Alexandria, VA: TESOL.

Hubbard, P. (2008). CALL and the future of language teacher education. *CALICO Journal*, *25*(2), 175–188.

Hubbard, P., & Levy, M. (2006). The scope of CALL education. In P. Hubbard & M. Levy (Eds.), *Teacher education in CALL* (pp. 3–20). Amsterdam: John Benjamins.

Kessler, G. (2006). Assessing CALL teacher training: What are we doing and what could we do better? In P. Hubbard & M. Levy (Eds.), *Teacher education in CALL* (pp. 23–42). Amsterdam: John Benjamins.

Kolb, D. A. (1984). *Experiential learning: Experience as the source of learning and development*. Upper Saddle River, NJ: Prentice Hall.

Lave, J., & Wenger, E. (1991). *Situated learning: Legitimate peripheral participation*. Cambridge: Cambridge University Press.

Mezirow, J. (2000). *Learning as transformation: Critical perspectives on a theory in progress*. San Francisco, CA: Jossey-Bass.

Newell, A., & Simon, H. A. (1972). *Human problem solving*. Englewood Cliffs, NJ: Prentice Hall.

Prensky, M. (2001). Digital natives, digital immigrants. Part 1. *On the Horizon*, *9*(5), 1–6. Retrieved from http://www.marcprensky.com/writing/Prensky%20-%20Digital%20Natives,%20Digital%20Immigrants%20-%20Part1.pdf

Salmon, G. (2011). *E-moderating: The key to teaching and learning online*. London: Routledge.

Son, J.-B. (2004). Teacher development in e-learning environments. In J.-B. Son (Ed.), *Computer-assisted language learning: Concepts, contexts and practices* (pp. 107–122). APACALL Book Series Volume 1. Lincoln, NE: iUniverse.

Son, J.-B. (2014). Moving beyond basics: From CALL coursework to classroom practice and professional development. In J.-B. Son (Ed.), *Computer-assisted language learning: Learners, teachers and tools* (pp. 122–149). APACALL Book Series Volume 3. Newcastle upon Tyne, UK: Cambridge Scholars Publishing.

TESOL (2008). *TESOL technology standards framework*. Alexandria, VA: TESOL. Retrieved from https://www.tesol.org/docs/books/bk_technologystandards_framework_721.pdf

Williams, M., & Burden, R. L. (1997). *Psychology for language teachers: A social constructivist approach*. Cambridge: Cambridge University Press.

Woodward, T. (2003). *Models and metaphors in language teacher training: Loop input and other strategies*. Cambridge: Cambridge University Press.

Appendix A

An Overview of the CALL Training Courses Presented in the Book

	Chapter 2	Chapter 3	Chapter 4	Chapter 5	Chapter 6	Chapter 7	Chapter 8	Chapter 9	Chapter 10
Course title	**SLAT7860 Language and Technology**	**LING90006 Technology and Language Learning**	**LIN8006 Computer-Assisted Language Learning**	**EDUC 7006 Language Learning and Technology**	**TESP005 Introduction to CALL**	**ALT8016 Computer-Assisted Language Learning**	**LING 5510 Computers in Language Teaching**	**GSL520 Computer-Assisted Language Learning Online**	**Linguistics 191/291 CALL Mini-Course**
University	University of Queensland, Australia	University of Melbourne, Australia	University of Southern Queensland, Australia	University of Manchester, UK	University of Stirling, UK	Newcastle University, UK	Ohio University, USA	Saint Michael's College, USA	Stanford University, USA
Mode	On-campus	On-campus; online	On-campus; online	On-campus; online	On-campus	On-campus	On-campus; online	Online	On-campus; materials available online to all
Objectives	1. Critically evaluate the literature on new technologies and language learning. 2. Locate and evaluate various CALL applications effectively. 3. Design and develop language learning materials underpinned by CALL principles. 4. Identify and apply the pedagogical opportunities of mobile technologies and the internet.	– Understand the theoretical basis for the use of technology in second language teaching. – Be able to critically assess and evaluate the role of technology in second language learning. – Appreciate a range of approaches to research focused on technology in second language learning.	On successful completion of this course, students will be able to: 1. demonstrate a basic understanding of second language teaching methodology in relation to computer technology; 2. show an awareness of research directions in CALL; 3. identify language teachers' roles in CALL contexts;	This unit aims to: – foster an awareness of developments in technology assisted language learning and its relationship with language teaching and learning and broader educational research. – develop advanced knowledge and understanding of the role(s) of technology in language teaching and learning in the light of relevant research, theory and issues of debate. – enable students to develop the necessary skills and understanding to use a range of technologies in their practice.	Students will: 1. Be familiar with the main trends in the historical development of CALL. 2. Be familiar with the use of the internet for language teaching for teacher-fronted, self-access and distance modes. 3. Be familiar with the learning theories relevant to the design, use and evaluation of CALL software. 4. Have a critical awareness and understanding of the relevance of second language learning theory to the design and use of CALL software.	– To introduce computer-based resources that can be used for language learning. – To understand some of the major advantages and limitations of using computer-based resources for language learning. – To understand how computer-based resources can be integrated into language courses.	By the end of this course, students will be able to: 1. identify common and potential issues regarding CALL related decision-making; 2. create effective CALL materials; 3. collect and archive CALL materials; 4. understand current approaches to CALL implementation; 5. demonstrate the ability to introduce software for students;	– Establish an interactive and collaborative online learning community by using computer-mediated communication tools, including a learning management system (computer-mediated communication literacy); – Demonstrate their understanding of the history, theory and research of CALL;	The goal of the course is to provide a conceptual foundation to the many facets of the CALL field so that individuals can make informed decisions about what specific CALL projects they might like to pursue. It is linked to a subset of the TESOL Technology Standards.

	Chapter 2	Chapter 3	Chapter 4	Chapter 5	Chapter 6	Chapter 7	Chapter 8	Chapter 9	Chapter 10
Course title	**SLAT7860 Language and Technology**	**LING90006 Technology and Language Learning**	**LIN8006 Computer-Assisted Language Learning**	**EDUC 7006 Language Learning and Technology**	**TESP005 Introduction to CALL**	**ALT8016 Computer-Assisted Language Learning**	**LING 5510 Computers in Language Teaching**	**GSL520 Computer-Assisted Language Learning Online**	**Linguistics 191/291 CALL Mini-Course**
	5. Integrate CALL materials into language learning courses. 6. Identify basic CALL instructional design issues. 7. Identify and analyse research issues and findings in CALL.		4. demonstrate a knowledge of the practical uses of CALL in second language learning and teaching.	– enable students to critically evaluate the potential and specific application of technology with respect to different contextual factors: learner profiles and needs, predominant methodological paradigms, technological setting, cultural setting.	5. Have a critical understanding of the nature of computer-mediated communication. 6. Be able to identify, select and critically evaluate CALL software. 7. Have an understanding of the potential and limitations of the computers and IT in the language classroom. 8. Have an understanding of the roles of the teacher, the learner and the computer in the CALL class.	– To introduce basic design issues relevant to computer-based language learning materials. – To develop basic skills in producing computer-based language learning materials.	6. demonstrate the ability to evaluate software; 7. demonstrate the ability to use a course management system; 8. demonstrate proficiency with current software.	– Demonstrate competence in the use of computers and mobile devices as well as their applications for teaching, in particular language teaching (digital literacy); – Author instructional materials for their target learners that incorporate applications for computers and mobile devices for flipping the classroom, including multimedia, internet resources and web-based authoring tools (multimedia literacy); – Evaluate online information, resources and courseware critically (information literacy);	

Objectives								– Practice the learned technologies with their students by incorporating similar projects into their specific teaching and learning environments; – Identify and use online resources for professional development.	
Contents	– History to current perspectives; – CALL theory and design principles; – CALL evaluation; – Language skills and areas: What's available? – Affordances for writing; – Online tools: corpora and dictionaries; – Learner perspectives; – Culture and culture learning; – Mobile learning; – CALL Integration and normalisation; – Towards the future	Introduction, with a focus on normalisation and technology integration; Specific areas of technology use; Research approaches with technologies	Module 1. Background; Module 2. Research on CALL; Module 3. Language teachers in CALL environments	– Second language learning and the development of electronic literacy – The nature of reading in a digital world and the development of reading skills through the use of computer-based tasks and the WWW – Technology and task and text authenticity – Computer based and networked writing development – Language learning and Web 2.0 – Synchronous and asynchronous computer mediated communication for language learning – The impact of technology use on learner talk	9. Be familiar with methods and issues relevant to the teaching of reading, writing, listening and speaking. 10. Be familiar with the use of computers in the assessment of language proficiency. – History of CALL – Evaluation of online materials – Use of CMC – Multimedia theory in CALL – Online pedagogies for reading, writing, listening and speaking – Computer-based language assessment	– Identifying and evaluating web-based resources for language learning and teaching – Using web-based resources for communication and for practising language skills – Planning lessons to integrate computer- and web-based resources into language courses – Designing and creating computer- and web-based resources for language learning	Introduction to CALL; Evolution of CALL; CALL trends – gaming; CMC in CALL; Multimedia for CALL; Social media in CALL; Evaluating materials; Feedback	1. Goals of the course and course project (a Wiki as a portfolio and LMS); CALL, blended learning, 21st-century technology skills; goals and history of CALL; literacies 2. Collaborating in an online environment; using presentation software for teaching and learning	8 Units – Introduction to computer-assisted language learning – Finding and evaluating CALL resources – Computer mediated communication – CALL and language skills – Environments, materials, and activities – CALL theory and research – Teacher education, professional development and learner training – Current trends and future directions

	Chapter 2	Chapter 3	Chapter 4	Chapter 5	Chapter 6	Chapter 7	Chapter 8	Chapter 9	Chapter 10
Course title	**SLAT7860 Language and Technology**	**LING90006 Technology and Language Learning**	**LIN8006 Computer-Assisted Language Learning**	**EDUC 7006 Language Learning and Technology**	**TESP005 Introduction to CALL**	**ALT8016 Computer-Assisted Language Learning**	**LING 5510 Computers in Language Teaching**	**GSL520 Computer-Assisted Language Learning Online**	**Linguistics 191/291 CALL Mini-Course**
				– The role of video texts in language learning – Computers and data driven learning – Digital games in language learning				3. Using the internet and mobile apps to support teaching and learning in language areas 4. Evaluating CALL resources 5. Project-based learning and teaching 6. Using concordancing for teaching and learning 7. Gaming in teaching and learning 8. Authoring content to support teaching and learning in all language areas; 9. Electronic assessment and gradebooks 10. Communities of Practice: online professional development resources and strategies	
Text and readings	Recommended texts and online readings	Recommended texts and online readings	No prescribed text; online readings	A variety of books and articles	Recommended texts and online sources	Recommended texts and online readings	No prescribed text; online readings	No prescribed text; online readings	Text online at http://web.stanford.edu/~efs/callcourse2

	Chapter 2	Chapter 3	Chapter 4	Chapter 5	Chapter 6	Chapter 7	Chapter 8	Chapter 9	Chapter 10
Workload	1 Semester (13 weeks)	1 Semester (12 teaching weeks) – lectures, seminars and workshops (33 hours); independent study (177 hours)	1 Semester (15 weeks) – directed study (80 hours) and independent study (80 hours)	1 Semester 15 weeks – 45 contact hours + independent study and assessment adding up to a nominal 150 hours	11 x 3 hr classes plus 66 hours of independent study.	1 Semester (12 teaching weeks) – lectures, seminars and workshops (32 hours); independent study (168 hours)	1 Semester (15 weeks)	1 Semester (15 weeks) – equivalent of 3 credits (37.5 hours + 75–112.5 hours); total 112.5–150 hours	8 weeks of a 10-week quarter
Assessment	Assignment 1 (20%) – Critical reflections (x2) on current CALL research articles Assignment 2 (35%) Critical evaluation – (a) evidence-based rationale for evaluation; (b) design of evaluation tool; (c) practical use of evaluation tool on three CALL websites / applications Assignment 3 (45%) Podcasting project – (a) create five-minute podcast for language learners or teachers; (b) 1000w evidence-based rationale, including an overview of instructional programme and the place of this podcast	An essay of 3500 words on self-directed topic to total 70%, due at the end of semester Regular participation in online discussions available in the subject LMS site, totalling 1500 words to total 30%	Assignment 1 – literature review (25%) and discussion forums (25%); Assignment 2 – evaluation report (40%) and discussion group postings (10%)	(1) Description of a teaching context and technology provision – approx. 500 words (approx. 10%) (2) A review of research into the use of technology identified in Part (1), identifying potentials and challenges from the research. Up to 2500 words (approx. 80%); a practical demonstration of understanding of how the technology identified might be applied in the context outlined in (1), taking account of the findings outlined in (2) (3) Lesson plan and/or teaching materials with brief commentary highlighting salient features – approx. 500 words (approx. 10%)	Mid-semester assignment: An evaluation of an online language learning resource (1750 words, 50%) Final assignment: Take-away test (1500 words, 50%)	Essay (50%) Computer/web-based language learning materials (50%)	Materials creation (10%); Leading discussion (20%); Collaborative midterm (30%); Curricular design project (40%)	– Reading Discussion Forum (15%) – Sharing What You Learned Discussion Forum (15%) – Moderating (10%) – Interactive / Collaborative tasks (5%) – Hands-on Projects (30%) – Collaborative web site review (10%) – Wiki portfolio web space for teaching and learning (15%) – Extra credit (2%)	Final project in-class presentation and paper
Other requirements	No prerequisite	No prerequisite	No prerequisite; regular internet access	Some background in teaching languages	No prerequisite	No prerequisite	No prerequisite; regular internet access	Basic computing skills; regular computer and internet access	Preparation of weekly assignments for discussion

2

Language and Technology

Theory and Practice, Options and Issues in Computer-Assisted Language Learning

Mike Levy and Paul J. Moore
The University of Queensland, Australia

Introduction

The computer-assisted language learning (CALL) course (titled 'Language and Technology') presently being offered at the University of Queensland has enjoyed a long period of incubation and development passing through numerous iterations and permutations since the original course was offered by the first author at Bond University in 1990. Yet while there have been numerous changes, there have been some underlying principles that have remained relatively stable. For example, the course content has always been largely determined through a three-pronged attack: the prevailing learning and teaching theories; the technologies in use; and the students' background and needs. The majority of course participants have always been international students from many parts of the world coming to an Australian university to study. After their studies, the majority return to their countries of origin to work as university academics and language teachers. Thus, while the goals of the course may respond to the latest developments in language learning research and pedagogy and the latest in technological resources, the teachers and coordinators also keep firmly in mind the educational contexts within which the students will ultimately be working. Obviously, the very latest innovations to create effective language learning environments are presented, and a wide range of options are considered, but this does not mean that student perspectives, and their goals are forgotten.

Another relative constant relates to the basic sequence of assessment items adopted in the course. Three successive assessment items build upon one another as they become progressively more complex and demanding. These items begin with the students intensively reading the literature, then a detailed, criteria-driven evaluation assignment and finally to a materials development project. The first item, through extensive reading, requires a critical reflection of what has already been achieved in CALL – and what has not. The evaluation stage looks at a wide range of CALL materials and learning environments and considers the appropriate criteria (theory and/or practice-driven) to evaluate them. The materials development stage involves the creation of some CALL materials (from websites to multimedia presentations to podcast and vodcasts) following by an empirical evaluation and some self-reflections on the development process and what has worked and what has not. Thus, the overall goal, by the end of the course, is that students have a thorough introduction to the theory and practice of CALL through the development of knowledge and practical skills that they can apply in their future teaching contexts.

Context

The Language and Technology course is part of the coursework postgraduate programme in applied linguistics. The Master of Applied Linguistics requires three semesters of full-time or part-time equivalent study, and typically students take four courses per semester. The programme offers a range of courses in the linguistic, psychological, educational and sociocultural aspects of language learning and use, and in language teaching methodology. The programme enables students to develop an advanced understanding of the field and to undertake research training through a coursework dissertation (one semester full-time). Many of the dissertations are in the area of CALL.

The programme is situated in the School of Languages and Cultures in the Faculty of Humanities and Social Sciences. The School specializes in teaching and research in Chinese, Japanese, Korean, Indonesian, Spanish, French, German and Russian languages and cultures, and in linguistics and applied linguistics. It is quite common for faculty in these language-teaching areas – notably French – to supervise thesis students in the Applied Linguistics programme. Efforts are made to cross-fertilize according to an individual student's language background and interests, and where possible to accommodate specific goals in their research. Opportunities for collaboration among students and staff across areas within the School are explored and taken where relevant. In many ways the

Applied Linguistics programme serves as a 'hub' for networking and collaboration in research and teaching within the School, especially in domains such as teaching methodology, inter and cross-cultural communication and assessment. A proportion of the MA students who undertake a Master's level thesis go on to do a PhD.

Typically, students complete the Language and Technology course in their second semester. In the first semester students usually take the following courses: Introductory Concepts in Applied Linguistics; Second Language Teaching; Second Language Acquisition; and Research Methods. Thus, when the Language and Technology course comes around in the second semester, students will have received an introduction to core ideas and concepts. For the CALL course, this is especially relevant in relation to their understanding of SLA and pedagogical principles. The relationship between CALL and SLA is discussed later in the Features and Issues section.

The content and areas of focus are also inevitably informed by the research interests of the staff. There are effectively 3.5 staff in the Applied Linguistics programme and obviously all possible topics cannot be covered. The programme has a strong international profile in the following areas:

- Classroom second language acquisition
- Language processing
- Language testing and assessment
- Task-based language teaching, learning and assessment
- Technology-mediated language learning and use
- Social and cultural contexts of second language learning and use
- Vocabulary development and assessment

Through exposure to these topics in applied linguistics, through individual courses and the programme as a whole, the students are often drawn to these subject areas when they reach the stage of negotiating their thesis topics with supervisors.

Course description

Content

SLAT7860 is an introductory course of thirteen weeks duration (three hours per week) covering the role and function of digital technologies within the context of formal and informal language learning, inside and outside of the classroom. The course focuses on the area known as CALL. The term CALL is used in a broad sense – somewhat like applied linguistics – to encompass the application of new technologies to language learning in all its forms: Technology-Enhanced Language Learning (TELL), Network-Based Language Learning (NBLL), Information and Communication Technologies (ICTs) for language learning, Mobile-Assisted Language Learning (MALL) and so on.

Study of the literature on CALL is integrated with the use and critical evaluation of a wide range of technologies and applications. These range across platforms (e.g., an institutional learning management system (LMS), desktops, laptops, tablets, smart phones) and types of application (e.g., websites, authentic materials, commercially produced language learning courseware, authoring programmes, webquests and apps). Spread across these applications, students will look at language-specific materials (e.g., online dictionaries, concordancers, automatic translators) as well as generic software used or customized for the purposes of language learning (e.g., off-the-shelf games). Studies of more socially oriented CALL, via blogs, wikis and telecollaboration, for example, are explored to raise students' awareness of the potential cultural, social and linguistic opportunities and challenges of online learning communities.

Relevant theories, principles and models are explored through readings, group discussion, and through demonstrations of CALL activities and learning environments. At the end of the course, students should be able to locate, evaluate and use CALL materials, and they should have developed an appreciation of the issues involved in designing and creating their own CALL activities, evaluating materials and effectively integrating them into language teaching and learning programmes.

Week by week

The breakdown of the weekly topics and themes is given below. While clearly it is not possible to elaborate on all the detail, some of the central concepts and ideas are discussed together with some comments on the overall structure and sequencing.

1. Introduction
2. History: 1950s to current contexts
3. Theoretical perspectives on CALL: From principles to practice
4. Evaluation
5. Computer-mediated communication and communities of practice

6. Language skills and areas
7. Reading and writing: Tools and processes
8. Concordances and dictionaries
9. Culture learning
10. Mobile learning
11. Learner perspectives
12. Integration
13. Future

In the Introduction, Gartner's 'Hype Cycle' is discussed to alert students to the transient nature of consumer technologies in the modern world (Gartner, 2014). Gartner's five phases of technology adoption (or rejection) – innovation trigger, peak of inflated expectations, trough of disillusionment, slope of enlightenment, plateaux of productivity – are helpful in understanding patterns of development, adoption and use. It is against this background of continuing change, and to some extent fashion, that students are compelled to work after they complete the MA programme. Various modes of learning are introduced and discussed too, such as blended learning and flipped learning. As a way of grounding the discussion, a particular research example is given showing the results of a survey of language students' goals and motivations. Thus student needs and goals are established as a key reference point when contemplating any use of new technology in language learning. In the first week, students are also introduced to the idea that learning a language requires attention to the development across a range of skills and areas, and that new technologies can help in different ways for each of them (e.g., vocabulary-electronic dictionaries-smart phone; see Levy, 2009).

An understanding of the historical context of CALL is built largely upon a comparison between CALL in the 1950s and 1960s through to the present day, though with an acknowledgement of the book (the printed word) and what it represents as a long-standing technological resource for language learning. From the former comfortable alliance among linguistics (structuralism), psychology (behaviourism) and pedagogy (audiolingualism) that led to the widespread introduction of language laboratories and language practice drills, the students explore the ways in which the different theoretical perspectives have evolved and changed through to the present day. The goal here is to appreciate the continuing evolution of the field, and in some respects its instability as far as technology is concerned, leading to a deeper understanding of student use of new technologies in the modern world. To support the discussion, a timeline is presented showing the time at which key technologies or applications were introduced. Students are regularly surprised when shown the recency of applications that they now consider fully integrated into modern life. References to the literature on the historical stages of CALL are also brought into the conversation, such as Kern and Warschauer (2000) and the critical response by Bax (2003). Of course, our personal experience as CALL educators is also drawn on at relevant stages to bring this history to life.

The historical perspective includes some discussion of theory in relation to practice, and this topic is taken up in more detail the following week. The majority of students completed the SLA course the previous semester, so in this course the teacher can focus on the application of the different theories in the different areas of CALL. The connection between SLA and CALL is discussed at length – this topic is returned to later in the 'Features and Issues' section. Reference is made to relevant, influential works that relate theory to technology use: included here are the conditions for optimal language learning environments (Egbert, Chao, & Hanson-Smith, 1999), Levy's tutor/tool distinction (Levy, 1997), and Chapelle's principles of evaluation and her criteria for task appropriateness (Chapelle, 2001). The first few weeks aim to give students a solid overview of the field including some of the prevailing forces in development and use, a historical context and an indication of how different theoretical perspectives relate to practice. During these early weeks, the students are expected to do a considerable amount of reading on CALL. This coincides with the requirements of the first assignment, two critical reflections of CALL research studies in one of the CALL journals (worth 10% each).

We now move to the more practical issue of evaluation by first looking at how a language textbook might be evaluated before expanding the ideas for other technology-mediated materials and resources. Theory still plays a role, but the emphasis here is to look closely and in-depth at a range of technology-mediated language learning resources ranging from websites to dictionaries and the like. This topic also relates directly to the first major assignment where the students are required to choose a technology and a language learning focus (e.g., vocabulary app/mobile phone) and to develop sound criteria for an evaluation (see assessment section). Students are challenged to get under the surface of the superficial appeal of a particular technology or application and develop concrete principles in order to assess its value. Though a little dated now, the Murray and Barnes (1998) article 'Beyond the "wow" factor' very much captures the intent of this activity. Chapelle's (2001) Judgemental/Empirical evaluation framework is discussed, and a range of other approaches and methods are also covered.

Evaluation is also the theme of the second assignment (worth 35%). This evaluation assessment comprises three stages. Stage 1 requires the student to select a technology/language learning focus and to write a rationale for the evaluation in essay style. Stage 2 requires the student to prepare specific evaluation criteria, logically following on from what he/she has said in the essay in Stage 1; this part is presented as an evaluation form or checklist. Stage 3 requires the student to complete (i.e., actually fill in) his/her form or checklist for three websites, software packages, or language learning environments.

The following week students are taken deeper into the nature of online interactions, and distinctions are made between online and face-to-face, both in CALL research studies and in practice. Contemporary synchronous and asynchronous technologies are compared and contrasted particular in terms of the nature of the interaction and the potential for language learning. Actual study results are used comparing email interactions with chat for example. The notion of affordances is also introduced in this context as asynchronous technologies such as email lend themselves more to an interaction where students have time to reflect on their input compared with synchronous interactions such as text chat or Skype where more immediate responses are required. A connection between these technologies and the competing needs of the learner for a focus on complexity, accuracy and fluency are discussed, as is the need to develop both speaking and writing skills. At a deeper level, issues of interface design are also examined as in the two stages that text chat is created, privately first (with the option to edit), then publicly. Thus, text chat is not synchronous in the way that face-to-face conversation is synchronous; the differences and the implications for learning are thoroughly explored. Conversation Analysis is also introduced to show the ways in which the detail of the interaction can be uncovered.

The next topic on the language skills and areas further elaborates on such recurring themes as a technology's affordances and the alignment of skill (speaking, listening, reading, writing, culture) or area (pronunciation, grammar, vocabulary, discourse) with a specific technology (see Chapelle & Jamieson, 2008). Breaking the skills and areas down into elements in this way helps to give an idea of how different language learning goals might align with the use of a specific technology with particular affordances. It also shows the breadth (and depth) of a field like CALL. More specifically, a more detailed examination is given of the nature of the listening skill, with reference to recent research into listening processes and pedagogy (e.g., Rost, 2011; Vandergrift, 2013), including affordances of multimedia (e.g., Plass & Jones, 2005). A range of well-known websites for listening are then reviewed and evaluated as well as a number of dedicated language-learning podcasts. This latter topic also gives an opportunity to introduce some of the concepts required for the final major assignment.

This discussion on the language skills and areas paves the way for the next four weeks which look in turn at: (1) reading and writing tools and processes; (2) concordances and dictionaries; and (3) culture learning; and (4) mobile learning. A few points are worth expanding here on these topics that are not immediately obvious, and all relate to a deeper examination of the topic and the technology. For example, students look closely at the wider capabilities of a well-known application like Word with a view to understanding lesser known multimedia capabilities such as sound and image. This is important because research shows that programmes such as Word and PowerPoint are very commonly used for language learning in schools where they should be exploited to their fullest extent (see Levy, 2012). The potential to customize the grammar checker is also explored. Here also reading on screen and on paper is contrasted, the influence of hyperlinks in reading online texts is considered, and E-ink is explained. Next the use of concordances and dictionaries is examined using data from the large-scale study by Levy and Steel (2015). This discussion shows study reports on such techniques as eye-tracking which indicate how a user reads a dictionary with incidental vocabulary learning. The whole notion of what comprises a modern online dictionary is considered and differences between mobile and desktop versions are examined. The link between technology and language learning is further considered in culture learning (see Levy, 2007). A very wide range of technologies and techniques are explored that variously facilitate culture learning in all its aspects with *Cultura* being presented as an exemplar (see Furstenberg, Levet, English, & Maillet, 2001). Finally, mobile learning and a wide variety of apps are examined with a particular focus again on vocabulary learning. The findings from research studies are again considered (Levy & Kennedy, 2005, 2008).

The final three lecture presentations aim to bring the strands together while pointing to the inevitable change to come, through a discussion of learner perspectives, integration (and normalisation) and the future. Taking its cue from Conole's (2008) article on listening to the learner's voice, the first session looks closely at learning a language through the eyes of the contemporary student. Where possible student data is used to inform the discussion and ways in which the students in the class use technologies is included. This relates also to their preferences and the ways in which they relate particular tasks (and people) to particular technologies and channels for interaction. It also incorporates not only the affordances of the technologies, but also the affordances of the hybrid discourses (e.g., academic and vernacular; see Murray, Hourigan & Jeanneau, 2011) and learning communities (e.g., Darhower, 2007) that emerge through online collaboration.

The number of alternative technologies in play, from the institution's LMS to the many personal technologies students might use on their smart phones leads to the question of integration. How do we pull together all the different strands so that language learners have a sense of continuity and coherence. This discussion includes the idea of normalisation (see Levy & Stockwell, 2006, for discussion), and the ways in which a typical textbook might be supplemented and extended to create a richer language learning environment that might provide more options to suit individual needs. The relation between in-class and out-of-class learning is also included. Finally, we reflect upon the future. With appropriate references, virtual worlds, gaming and machine translation (e.g., Google) are presented, and techniques such as augmented reality for language learners are described and illustrated. More importantly, we reflect upon the guidelines and principles that apply as we chart the way forward.

Features and issues

One of the principal features of the Language and Technology course throughout its life has been the parallel evolution of the course with the field of CALL as a whole, as an emerging field of specialist study. Developments and issues that have arisen in the broader context have echoed through the course such that new research methods and findings are discussed, and issues, as they arise, are revisited and debated at the local level. For example, the editorial in *Computer-Assisted Language Learning*, by Levy and Hubbard (2005), 'Why call CALL "CALL"' was hotly debated in class. Seminal articles by Chapelle, such as, 'CALL in the year 2000: Still in search of research paradigms' (Chapelle, 1997), and 'Is network-based learning CALL?' (Chapelle, 2000), also provided a basis for intense discussion. The point is that the course has always remained closely interlinked and engaged with the field as a whole, and students are always encouraged to read widely and to deeply engage with the current literature. This is considered essential, not only to keep abreast of developments in the field while students are enrolled in the Master's programme, but also to develop habits for the future. It is reasonable to assume that language teachers and practitioners of all kinds will confront numerous challenges in the future and it is important students are prepared.

This deep level of ongoing engagement with the literature extends to understanding the theories that influence CALL and the wide variety of applications of technology in language learning (see Levy & Hubbard, 2016). Of special note is the role of SLA in CALL. Students in Language and Technology have generally had an introduction to SLA in the previous semester so they are familiar with the major theories. Such theories can prove problematic in CALL if they are used prescriptively without full acknowledgement of the context of use, particularly as in technology-mediated communication rather than conventional face-to-face. Such issues have been discussed at some length with regard to SLA theory and research and its application. For example, Mitchell and Myles (2004), citing the work of Ellis (1997), report: 'The findings of SLA research are not sufficiently secure, clear and uncontested, across broad enough domains, to provide straightforward prescriptive guidance for the teacher (nor, perhaps, will they ever be so)' (Mitchell & Myles, 2004, p. 261). Even for the subfield of instructed SLA, they continue, 'instructed SLA research is not identical with problem-solving and development in language pedagogy, and does not ensure a shared agenda between teachers and researchers' (p. 262). On the other hand, Mitchell and Myles add that we should certainly not forget the value of this association: ' present SLA research offers a rich variety of concepts and descriptive accounts, which can help teachers interpret and make better sense of their own classroom experiences, and significantly broaden the range of pedagogic choices open to them' (p. 262). The same points, we believe, apply in CALL.

One complication for CALL when applying research findings from so-called mainstream cognitive SLA is the *assumption* that face-to-face communication is equivalent to technology-mediated communication, and that findings from research into one mode automatically apply to the other. Because of this assumption, O'Rourke (2008) argues that many aspects of the learning environment relevant to learning in synchronous CMC have been neglected, namely:

a) users' paralinguistic and non-linguistic behaviours – gestures, spoken utterances, posture etc.;
b) interactional tempo, both globally (whether a session is generally characterized by rapid or more leisurely exchanges) and locally (response latency, i.e., the length of gaps between particular turns);
c) drafting processes – i.e., editing of input prior to sending; and
d) attentional focus – i.e., what users are actually attending to at a given moment. (p. 233)

The assumption of equivalence is not made in the CALL course. Instead the default position is one of difference (until proven otherwise). As Levy (2000) observes: 'For the CALL researcher, technology always makes a difference; the technology is never transparent or inconsequential' (p. 190).

Care also has to be taken not to limit the field of view unnecessarily in considering CALL technologies. The diversity of CALL is immense with the potential to impact on all the language skills and areas from the design and development of dictionary apps to digital games through speech recognition to machine translation to artificial intelligence. If mainstream SLA were the only guide, then a focus in CALL that tended only towards telecollaboration projects would be the end result. While such projects are perfectly valid, they hardly account for the range of applications in CALL, nor the value of CALL for the independent, autonomous learner (see Guth & Helm, 2010). More importantly, technology tends to move forward in leaps and bounds, and preparedness for the future comes not from just knowing one approach, or how to make use of what exists in one area today. Students need to be exposed to a wide range of possibilities, and develop a keen sense of exploration across the areas of applied linguistics, language and new technologies so that they may be ready to adapt and absorb when new and sometimes unexpected innovations appear and enter the mainstream.

In discussing these more abstract issues, it should not be forgotten that CALL is also very much a practical course reflecting its origins as a design discipline. It is not just a matter of taking 'off-the-shelf' products and using them. It is also about creativity. Those in CALL have been designers, or 'makers' from the very beginnings and CALL materials development – from scratch, or to extend or fill in the gaps evident in a language textbook – is still very much part of a CALL practitioner's repertoire. We should say immediately that we do not teach computer programming, or anything like it, and we are keen to quickly dismiss any idea that students believe that they need to be able to program a computer to pass the course. But at the same time we are keen for students to be confident technology users and to attain a high level of competence, and a particular approach is taken.

This practical ability is developed especially through the final assessment project (worth 45%). Although this has changed over the years, it has always involved the creation of an artefact that stretches a student both in terms of their conceptual understanding and their technical skill. In earlier times this related to the creation of a language learning website. In the last four years, it has involved the creation of a 'podcast' or more accurately a sound file on language teaching/learning that the students have to create themselves. The students have a choice, either to design a podcast for teachers, or one for students. In each case, the students are presented with a scenario (see Appendix A). Following training in the workshop component of the course, students can use Audacity, GarageBand or similar to create their podcast. Students work individually and in groups through a carefully devised series of stages, involving a series of task deadlines with checks and balances, at each stage working towards their final product. In addition to the podcast itself, students produce a reflective essay, in which they discuss the process of developing the podcast (background research, underlying pedagogical approach, technical aspects), and outline the institutional and pedagogical context of their podcast, including a brief overview of related learner needs and where their individual podcast fits in a series of lessons.

Finally, research shows the critical importance of learner training if students are to use their technological resources effectively for language learning (see Hubbard, 2004). Without focussed training, students are left to their own devices and a process of trial and error. There is an important difference between the use of a technology for entertainment purposes and for learning purposes that may be disregarded. In the course, therefore, particularly in the workshop component, students are trained in ways that may be replicated when they themselves are in the situation of training their own students. Thus, the pedagogical approach is made visible and discussed such that course participants can understand the rationale and the ways in which they are being taught. Again techniques devised by Hubbard are employed, such as using a cyclical approach, collaborative debriefing and teaching general exploitation strategies.

Future directions

In our view, in contemplating the future one must return to the students, the theory and the technologies in use. But in addition to these fundamentals the field of CALL does place extra demands on the course designer in terms of the rate of technological innovation and change. It is relentless. Futurists, who work to plan scenarios for the years ahead, often use the PEST model (named somewhat ironically given the changes that ensue following a successful technological innovation) and consider the political, economic, social and technological dimensions of the change likely to be encountered (e.g., see Ringland, 1998). In the contemporary world this broader, more holistic perspective is essential. But it is also vital in practical terms because it helps ensure viability and relevance in the many different settings in which our students will be teaching languages. Some will be high-tech, some low-tech, some will use state-of-the-art pedagogical approaches, some will follow more traditional practices. But in all settings, teachers will need to be sensitive to these prevailing influences and be able to adapt accordingly.

Aside from these broader considerations, our understandings of CALL will grow, as will our knowledge of how a language is taught and learnt. The idea of using technology in some form to extend a learner's time on task and to motivate and enrich the learning experience is important. Blended learning, flipped learning and mobile learning all require knowledgeable technology use if they are to be effective and live up to expectations (the hype?) about how they are set to improve language learning. Finally, there is no doubt that research in machine translation, augmented reality, speech recognition, artificial intelligence and so on will impact in various ways on our agendas. Some of these advances may penetrate deeply into language education, others may be more superficial and transient, as Gartner's analysis suggests. In this world of change, the stance we advocate is always to encourage a critical distance and a level-headed evaluation of the options, thus dismissing the 'hype' and avoiding the 'wow' factor, in both its positive and negative interpretations. Then, together with their newly acquired practical skills, we prepare students to meet the challenges they encounter in their future professional lives with confidence.

References

Bax, S. (2003). CALL – past, present, future. *System, 31*, 13–28.

Chapelle, C. A. (1997). CALL in the year 2000: Still in search of research paradigms? *Language Learning & Technology, 1*(1), 19–43.

Chapelle, C. A. (2000). Is network-based learning CALL? In M. Warschauer & R. Kern (Eds.), *Network-based language teaching: Concepts and practice* (pp. 204–228). Cambridge: Cambridge University Press.

Chapelle, C. A. (2001). *Computer applications in second language acquisition: Foundations for teaching, testing and research.* Cambridge: Cambridge University Press.

Chapelle, C. A., & Jamieson, J. (2008). *Tips for teaching with CALL: Practical approaches to CALL.* White Plains, NY: Pearson Education.

Conole, G. (2008). Listening to the learner voice: The ever-changing landscape of technology use for language students. *ReCALL, 20*(2), 124–140.

Darhower, M. (2007). A tale of two communities: Group dynamics and community building in a Spanish-English telecollaboration. *CALICO Journal, 24*(3), 561–589.

Egbert, Joy, Chao, C., & Hanson-Smith, E. (1999). Computer-enhanced language learning environments: An overview. In J. Egbert & E. Hanson-Smith (Eds.), *CALL Environments: Research, practice & critical issues* (pp. 1–13). Alexandria, VA: TESOL.

Ellis, R. (1997). *SLA research and language teaching*. Oxford: Oxford University Press.

Furstenberg, G., Levet, S., English, K. & Maillet, K. (2001). Giving a virtual voice to the silent language of culture: The *Cultura* project. *Language Learning & Technology, 5*(1), 55–102.

Gartner (2014). Hype cycle for emerging technologies maps the journey to digital business. Retrieved from http://www.gartner.com/newsroom/id/2819918

Guth, S., & Helm, F. (Eds.). (2010). *Tellecollaboration 2.0: Language, literacies and intercultural learning in the 21st century*. Bern: Peter Lang.

Hubbard, P. (2004). Learner training for effective use of CALL. In S. Fotos & C. Browne (Eds.), *New perspectives in CALL for second language classrooms* (pp. 45–67). Mahwah, NJ: Lawrence Erlbaum.

Kern, R., & Warschauer, M. (2000). Introduction: Theory and practice of network-based language teaching. In M. Warschauer & R. Kern (Eds.). *Network-based language teaching: Concepts and practice* (pp. 1–19). Cambridge: Cambridge University Press.

Levy, M. (1997). *Computer-assisted language learning: Context and conceptualization*. Oxford: Clarendon Press.

Levy, M. (2000). Scope, goals and methods in CALL research: Questions of coherence and autonomy. *ReCALL, 12*(2), 170–195.

Levy, M. (2007). Culture, culture learning and new technologies: Towards a pedagogical framework. *Language Learning & Technology, 11*(2): 104–127.

Levy, M. (2009). Technologies in use for second language learning. *The Modern Language Journal, 93*, 769–782.

Levy, M. (2012). Technology-enhanced language learning (TELL) in independent schools Queensland. A report prepared for ISQ. Brisbane, Queensland: ISQ.

Levy, M. (2015). The role of qualitative approaches to research in CALL: Rationale, choice and implementation. In R. Hampel & U. Stickler (Eds.), From second language acquisition to second language use: Qualitative and mixed method approaches to research in CALL today. *CALICO Journal*, Special Issue, *32*(2), September, 2015.

Levy, M., & Hubbard, P. (2005). Why call CALL 'CALL'? Editorial. *Computer Assisted Language Learning, 18*(3), 143–149.

Levy, M., & Hubbard, P. (2016). Theory in computer-assisted language learning research and practice. In L. Murray & F. Farr (Eds.), *Handbook of language learning and technology* (pp. 24–38). Oxford: Routledge.

Levy, M., & Kennedy, C. (2005). Learning Italian via mobile SMS. In A. Kukulska-Hulme & J. Traxler (Eds.), *Mobile technologies for teaching and learning*. ODL series. (pp. 76–83). London: Kogan Page/Taylor & Francis.

Levy, M., & Kennedy, C. (2008). L'italiano al teleonino: Using SMS to support beginners' language learning. *ReCALL, 20*(3), 315–330.
Levy, M., & Steel, C. (2015). Language learner perspectives on the functionality and use of electronic language dictionaries. *ReCALL, 27*(2), 177–196. doi:10.1017/S095834401400038X
Levy, M., & Stockwell, G. (2006). *CALL dimensions: Options and issues in computer assisted language learning.* New York: Lawrence Erlbaum Associates.
Mitchell, R., & Myles, F. (2004). *Second language learning theories* (2nd ed.). London: Arnold.
Murray, L., & Barnes, A. (1998). Beyond the 'wow' factor – evaluating multimedia language learning software from a pedagogical viewpoint. *System, 26*, 249–259.
Murray, L., Hourigan, T., & Jeanneau, C. (2011). Blog writing integration for academic language learning purposes: Towards an assessment framework. *Ibérica, 14*, 9–32.
O'Rourke, B. (2008). The other C in CMC: What alternative data sources can tell us about text-based synchronous computer-mediated communication and language learning. *Computer Assisted Language Learning, 21*(3), 227–251.
Plass, J., & Jones, L. (2005). Multimedia learning in second language acquisition. In R. Mayer (Ed.), *The Cambridge handbook of multimedia learning* (pp. 467–488). New York: Cambridge University Press.
Ringland, G. (1998). *Scenario planning: Managing for the future.* Chichester, UK: John Wiley & Sons.
Rost, M. (2011). *Teaching and researching listening* (2nd ed.). Harlow: Pearson Education.
Vandergrift, L. (2013). Teaching listening. In C. A. Chapelle (Ed.), *The encyclopedia of applied linguistics* (pp. 5632–5639). West Sussex: Wiley-Blackwell.

Appendix A

Task Description: Choose Option A or Option B

Option A: A podcast designed for language teachers

Scenario: A local radio station has asked you to develop a short podcast for a regular show based around the theme 'Teachers, learners and technology'. They want something that is informative and engaging that showcases the potential of a particular technology (or technologies) of your choice that is also practical for listeners who may be thinking of doing something similar. It is also important that you highlight the affordances of the technologies for different language skill and knowledge areas as well as holistically. They will be advertising the show to various language teacher networks nationally.

Option B: A podcast designed for language students

Scenario: You are teaching an intermediate/advanced language class and you have been requested by the Head of School to develop a series of weekly podcasts for this class to help them develop their listening skills. You are required to produce one podcast only as a sample. This podcast may be one from the beginning, middle or end of semester. You may specify more precisely the needs of your students and their goals and objectives.

3

Blended Approaches to Teaching Languages with Computers

Paul Gruba
University of Melbourne, Australia

Introduction

Educational technologies increasingly influence the way languages are taught, learned and assessed. Despite their own familiarity with many new technologies, early career modern language teachers are often challenged by the theories and practices that underlie contemporary computer-assisted language learning (CALL). In particular, they may become unsettled by the disappearance of technologies into blended language programmes, and be wary of goals that seek to develop new literacies and reconsider the tenets of traditional language assessment.

In this chapter, I set out my designs in the graduate course LING90006 Technology and Language Learning. I begin by providing context, and then I describe the course and set out the overall syllabus. I continue with a discussion of course features, and some of the issues that have arisen over the years, and conclude with a view of future developments.

Context

The University of Melbourne, established in 1853, is a large urban research university that often promotes itself as one of the best in Australia. The university consists of nine faculties, and undergraduate studies offer courses to complete one of six broad based degree programmes. The university is now set to expand its graduate degree programmes, with an increasing emphasis on coursework programmes, including those offered in the Faculty of Arts.

The Master of Applied Linguistics is one of fourteen coursework programmes that are offered through the Graduate School of Humanities and Social Sciences, Faculty of Arts. Within the degree programme, the course that I coordinate 'LING90006 Technology and Language Learning, is the core requirement for the 'Technology and Language Learning' stream that is one of five possible options for students. The other streams are Teaching English to Speakers of Other Languages (TESOL), Language Testing, English Language, and Modern Languages. Of these streams, TESOL is the most popular choice. Students are required to take one compulsory subject and one core subject. Students who elect to take the 'Technology and Language Learning' stream are required to complete a research methodology course as well as six other electives.

Students apply for the Master's degree from around the world, with the bulk of applications coming from Chile, China, Korea, Saudi Arabia and Singapore. To be eligible, students must have completed an undergraduate degree with above-average results. The default offer is for students to enter the two-year, 200-point option that consists of both introductory and advanced courses; if they have at least two years of related work experience, they are able to enter the one-year 100-point degree programme that is wholly made up of advanced courses. Each course unit is weighted 12.5 points, and students can elect to complete the programme either part-time or full-time. Our Master of Applied Linguistics programme is offered in blended mode such that the advanced courses can be taken on-campus, partially on-campus or entirely online through access to lecture and seminar recordings as well as course materials from a common learning management system (LMS). Accordingly, each session of the subject is recorded live and online participation is encouraged. Doctoral students can attend classes if they wish to do so.

Course description

At the University of Melbourne, we have two semesters a year and each consists of twelve weeks. In graduate programmes, courses meet for two hours per week; one hour is designated for a lecture and the second hour is intended for interactive seminars and group discussion.

Over the twelve-week semester, I divide my syllabus into three themes: (1) Introduction and key trends, (2) skills and technologies and (3) research and evaluation. Before discussing each of those themes with students, I first explain the assessment tasks and criteria. Perhaps unique in my School, I set participation in the discussion board to be 30 per cent of the total mark. The remainder of the final mark consists of writing an academic paper, either individually or in small groups, using the template for manuscript submission to a conference. The template requires students to identify their institutional affiliation, write an abstract and set key words. Importantly, they must also adhere to style guidelines (APA, 6th edition) and stay within word limits.

The first theme, an introduction to key trends in technology and language learning, begins with a brief history. I highlight the definition of CALL as 'a dynamic complex in which technology, theory, and pedagogy are inseparably interwoven' (Garrett, 2009, p. 720). Defined in this way, I stress the point that Garrett makes that CALL is not simply the 'use of technology' but rather a principled integration of technologies into a multilayered educational ecosystem; in this perspective, we look for the reasons that may underpin decisions to do with the allocation of resources in an area of limited funding.

Our early discussions bring out questions concerning the overall goal of modern language teaching. In my contribution to such discussions, I draw on the work of Blommaert (2010) and Kramsch (2014), for example, to remind us about the growing impact of globalization in language teaching and use. I point out that networked technologies are playing a major role in shifting definitions of language skills and pedagogical purposes, and indeed, stress the point that specialists in educational technologies and new media must remain particularly aware of their own contested roles in twenty-first century language education (e.g., Pennycook, 2008).

The next key point that I make is to emphasize an agenda for normalization of technologies as initially set out by Bax (2003), and that was fully articulated in work by Chambers and Bax (2006). In their article, Chambers and Bax identify four areas of concern – logistics, stakeholders, integration and training – as they suggest a need for no less than eleven fundamental changes that can lead to an improved use of technology in language programmes. Here, I slow down the pace of the lecture so that we have time to think about the practical issues in making suggested changes. With the article now a decade old, have such changes been enacted in ways that are transparent and visible in any of the students' local programmes – or, indeed, at the modern languages programmes at institutions as large and well-funded as those that are at the University of Melbourne? Our discussions often revolve around the embedded hierarchies of academic institutions, as well as a lack of professional development, that may slow the pace of innovation in modern language programmes (Waters, 2009).

During this early part of the semester, I also introduce the *TESOL Technology Standards* (Healey et al., 2008) as well as the New Media Consortium 'Horizon Report' for that year [nmc.org]. As I introduce the *Standards*, I hold them up to be an aspirational goal; that is, I present them to the students as a way for organizations to strive to put in place a clear set of articulated aims that can act as a catalyst for change and innovation. By discussing the *Standards* with colleagues, I suggest, it could help provide a roadmap for short and long-term development. I further push that need to innovate with technologies by introducing the Horizon Report. Though intended for mainstream education, the Horizon Report is a useful source for all of us to see technologies are currently being enacted, and what is those that are predicted to appear within the next three to five years ahead.

As part of my own response to the agenda for normalization, I introduce the notion of 'blended learning' that ostensibly seeks to establish a middle ground among those who strongly advocate, and those who fairly discourage, the use of technologies (Gruba & Hinkelman, 2012). Modern language educators have long blended materials and technologies in their courses, and so the idea is a familiar one, but here we seek to justify why technologies are integrated in contemporary programmes at all. Finally, to finish off in the third week, I introduce in a lecture what adopting a 'new literacies' agenda may mean to modern language teachers (Lotherington & Jenson, 2011). I highlight the point that the new literacies agenda has the potential to destabilize embedded and traditional views of the four major language skills. In the hour-long seminar that follows, we discuss the implications of blending and new literacies within the students' own varied educational systems and environments. Often, my students highlight the realities of being a teacher in systems that struggle to meet the directives of national policies as well as their own students' strong desires to pass large-scale international language proficiency tests. Against such resistance, they argue, a push for 'new literacies' training for themselves, their colleagues and their students within the language classroom is often fanciful.

During the initial three weeks of the semester, I spend a significant amount of time introducing students to the LMS. At the University of Melbourne, we use a branded version of Blackboard™ (Blackboard, 2015). I am fully aware of the many controversies surrounding the choice of such a facility such as its proprietary code and commercial uses. Because of my awareness, I raise issues about the Blackboard LMS usage to do with licensing costs, the large-scale institutional management of enrolment records, student privacy and the security of academic records and online materials. Many students have not thought of what

Table 3.1 Seminar schedule, weeks 1–3

Week	Topic	Key message	Assigned readings
1	Introduction: History and pressing issues	CALL is a specialist subfield of applied linguistics, seeking to integrate teaching, assessment and research	Garrett, 2009
2	Normalisation and standards	Technologies are growing and disappearing; Standards set aspirational goals for language learning programmes and institutions	Chambers & Bax, 2006; *TESOL Technology Standards*; *NMC Horizon Report*
3	Blended approaches and new literacies	Integration of technologies in face-to-face settings is normal and expected; new literacies are upsetting traditional views of skills and purposes	Gruba & Hinkelman, 2012, Chapter 1; Lotherington & Jenson, 2011

it takes to manage a large computer facility at a large university; as part of their professional training, though, I stress that at some point they themselves are likely to enter management positions.

Unique at the university, students in my course are given LMS 'tutor' privileges that allow them to have full access to build a collective site. To spur development, I ask the students to act as if they are running a language school: What would they like their own students to be able to do online? All students are directed to the 'staff' page of the university where they can, just as academic faculty do, watch short video clips to learn how to use various tools. During the second hour of every week that I designate for small group work and discussion, they are asked to work together and learn tools. The only caveat in my instructions to the students is that they must incorporate assessment into their designs.

The second theme of the course explores the theory and practice of the traditional four skill areas, and ends with an emphasis on assessment practices. As I introduce this theme, we again reflect on the long-standing move towards 'new literacies' that was reinforced in work by Lotherington and Jenson (2011). Again, students are sceptical: often, in their educational systems and institutions, there is likely to be little motivation, training or the technologies to push for such a wholesale change in prevailing views of language skills that are set out in national policies and dictated by large-scale testing instruments. I respond with this point: despite such resistance in many countries, other areas are moving quickly as we have seen in the Horizon Report. Can the TESOL Standards in Technology be used as a point of departure, or perhaps as an aspirational goal for all of us concerned with technologies and language learning?

The topic of speaking through, and with, technologies starts the second theme for the semester. Students are familiar with interactive video-conferencing technologies such as Skype, and my role here is to draw their attention to their affordances and limitations. To do this, I take a screen shot of a Skype call and point out how participants are framed and how their actions may appear (e.g., Licoppe & Morel, 2012); that is, although video chatting may appear 'natural', interactions are mediated and hence understanding may require specific new literacies skills. We then move to a study that examines speaking in an immersive world, and through this, introduce an awareness of task designs (Jauregi, Canto, de Graaff, Koenraad, & Moonen, 2011). In our classroom, that is full of computers, we then try to talk with each other through various mobile technologies, workstations and face to face; over the years, though, I have avoided getting accounts for immersive worlds such as *Second Life* as it tends to take too much time to set up and teach the basics. Our discussions concern the practicalities of speaking online including costs and account management.

Because mobility of the learner is a growing concern (Hulme, 2009), we also consider how smart phones may be used to teach speaking. Colleagues working in agreed schedules and times, I argue, could reach a few of their language students per day as a way to encourage telephone skills and speaking. Conversations would neither be formal nor assessed, but would focus on brief friendly exchanges that highlight the use of language for social and pragmatic purposes. I introduce this idea to bring out issues of workload and privacy, too, because networked technologies can also bring an unwelcome expectation of 24/7 interaction and connectivity.

Our next topic area explores mobile and online reading. My background, partially in media studies, follows Kress and van Leeuwen (2006), for example, to see 'reading' as the ability to make sense of words, static images and dynamic media within a coherent text or single site. To begin discussions, we pull up a current news site and take a quick inventory of what is required to make meaning of the range of material that appears. From headlines to news stories, from reader comments to monitor responses, from audio and video clips, we discuss how the language learner may struggle to make sense of a society in conversation. Through this activity, we see that reading cannot be seen simply as a skill that requires the decoding of words printed in black and white on a set page. We then focus on reading on mobile phones (Wang & Smith, 2013) that is so much part of the contemporary media landscape. Issues of privacy, too, are brought up as they were by Wang and Smith (2013). Discussions that week, both in-class and online, focus on the implications of what such a view of reading may mean to modern language pedagogies, research and assessments.

Writing is always a popular topic in the course. Most students have experience with blogs, I have found, but very few have worked extensively with wikis or other forms of online collaborative writing tools. I introduce the topic through the work of Lund (2008), and that involves explaining Activity Theory (e.g., Gibbes & Carson, 2014) that is used to frame the actions, rules and community involvement in the collaboration. What often emerges in our discussions is that students are often unaware just how complex a wiki can be.

When it comes to exploring listening, I often discuss my own struggles to do research in this area of study. In applied linguistics, listening is the least researched of the major skills (Vadergrift, 2007); as I run this course, I do my best to encourage students to highlight listening in their own language classes, pedagogical designs and research agendas. I begin by deconstructing my own study and how I came to adopt 'play' as a central metaphor for work with multimodal texts (Gruba, 2006). Once again, new literacies and the changing nature of language learning come to the fore, and one push in this week is to see how differing modes of presentation may influence how we come to understand and assess skills (e.g., Wagner, 2010).

We then move to an effort to establish a framework for help options in online listening (Cardenas-Claros & Gruba, 2012). Created with multimedia resources and annotation features, professional materials for teaching listening skills (such as Longman) can provide listeners with access to assistance throughout the entire process of learning; despite such ready access, however, few listeners take advantage of the resources that are available at their fingertips. Accordingly, I remind my own students, that one part of teaching listening is to teach language students how to make full use of the technologies, all the while reminding them that effective listening is a rapid, active and ephemeral process that is often situated in a social cultural context.

As a way to conclude our examination of technologies within the teaching of the four traditional skills in language programmes, we turn our attention to assessment designs and practices. Kress (2009) sets out our first question for exploration: in twenty-first century education, characterized by globalisation, participation and new literacies, what counts as success?

By this time in the semester, I expect students to have made substantial progress on the collective LMS site that they are building for the imagined learning

Table 3.2 Seminar schedule, weeks 4–8

Week	Topic	Key message	Assigned readings
4	Speaking	Technologies, such as Skype, can be integrated into speaking exercises; *Second Life* as a case study and task designs	Jauregi, Canto, de Graaff, Koenraad, & Moonen (2011)
5	Reading	Online reading of material, from email to discussion boards to mash-up sites, demands critical thinking and digital literacy	Wang & Smith, 2013
6	Writing	Collaborative actions forged by wikis can be understood through social cultural activity theory	Lund, 2008
7	Listening	Understanding software for listening training; Video as a mode of presentation, as through YouTube, demands an awareness of multimodal elements	Cardenas-Claros & Gruba, 2012; Gruba 2006; Vandergrift, 2007
8	Assessment	Often set aside, assessment practices are crucial to the effectiveness of technology integration and overall programme goals	Gruba & Hinkelman, 2012, Chapter 4

school. To be frank, I often have to push them a bit at this point to reinvigorate their efforts as a large disparity arises between students who have been steadily learning the LMS tools and those who have not shown much effort. Discussions arise about self-directed learning, or the goal of a graduate degree, and indeed, about the value of learning about a large-scale facility that may, or may not, have direct application to their own professional contexts.

In the third theme, we look at three research approaches in CALL: cognitive interactionist, social constructivist and action research. As a way to introduce this theme, I introduce the theme through work that paints a rather sombre view of the quality of research in our field (e.g., Burston, 2015; Golonka et al., 2012).

We start the first one with a review of second language acquisition principles, and highlight how the computer can be used to interact individually, in small groups, or across global networks. (Most of the students in the MA programme take a course in second language acquisition as part of their degree.) Work from Chapelle (2001) helps us to place technologies and task in interactionist theories, and we follow through those discussions by looking at social interactions in digital gaming (Cornillie, Thorne, & Desmet, 2012). Exploring action research is the most popular topic of the semester as judged by the large number of postings on the discussion board for the week. Its popularity, I think, is partially caused by the fact that our Master's programme in research methods does not cover action research, but also because the topic motivates students to inspire each other about areas to investigate in their own classrooms.

The lecture series ends with the final week devoted to the theme of persistent issues and future directions. Our final reading, in a way, is to reflect on topics that Chapelle (1997) outlined nearly two decades ago concerning the need for empirical studies, second language acquisition principles as a basis for CALL and evaluation. We look at Garrett (2009), again, too, and wonder to what extent our area needs to remain a distinct area of enquiry in applied linguistics and TESOL. Our week ends with the video recording of Chapelle (2014) giving a keynote presentation on programme evaluation in CALL, and then moves with a discussion of the thinking behind a book that I co-authored on blended language programme evaluation (Gruba, Cardenás-Claros, Suvorov, & Rick, 2016).

To end the semester, students are asked to give a brief presentation of their development of the LMS. By this time, the students have formed small teams to create a section of the collective site. In the past years, the results have been impressive: using the facility, they have created fully articulated sites that have been roughly divided into areas corresponding to the four skills. Their presentations must provide a context for the work, the targeted level of proficiency and demonstrate how the online learning module incorporates an assessment of learning. Of interest, the students often tie the LMS facility to the use of a commercial software tool; for example, they argue that the LMS is to be seen as a point of departure, or gateway, for a language lesson that will be grounded in video-sharing through YouTube, for example. It is often my insistence on the need to monitor and assess learning that drives LMS usage as the learning analytics and tools there can be used to justify development time, the integration of technology into the curriculum and promote reuse by colleagues.

Features and issues

My subject has three key features: an emphasis on the development of critical thinking through participation, full training in the use of the LMS and focus on research and theory development throughout the semester.

Table 3.3 Seminar schedule, weeks 9–12

Week	Topic	Key message	Assigned readings
9	Cognitive focused approaches	CALL, as with applied linguistics overall, has a long history of cognitivist-interaction research	Chapelle, 2001
10	Social constructivist approaches	Investigations centred in social views and interaction must take into account many factors	Cornillie, Thorne, & Desmet (2012)
11	Action research	Individuals and small groups can investigate local issues to create evidence to support warrants for programme change	Gruba & Hinkelman, 2012, Chapter 5
12	Programme evaluation and the disappearing future of CALL	CALL programmes need greater scrutiny through evaluation; The pervasive use of convergent technologies is sure to mainstream issues that were once the domain of specialists	Chapelle, 1997; Chapelle, 2014; Gruba, Cardenas-Claros, Survorov, & Rick, 2016

Based on a social constructivist view that learning takes place through interaction, I require students to participate throughout the semester within the online discussion board. Such participation accounts for 30 per cent of their total mark. Over the years, requiring students to participate so much in the course has been the subject of debate. In other course units, they remind me, there is little or no requirement to interact with other students: assessment is often counted through a set of 'homework' exercises, two written papers, and a brief in-class presentation. Why, then, is the discussion board in this course worth so much?

My response to such debate is that I have long 'located' myself in the landscape of educational technology as a social constructivist and that the adoption of such an approach has had implications for my own pedagogical design and assessment practices. Indeed, as applied linguists and other educators move increasingly towards social cultural views of language learning, what counts as proficiency must go beyond the current metrics of success to other forms of recognized achievement (Kress, 2009).

As I say to my students, knowing how to use the LMS effectively is a key requirement for anyone seeking a teaching position in higher education. Many of the students who come to the course however love to use and promote specialist tools such as those that can allow microblogging, instant photo sharing or developing narratives through pictures. Students from low-resource contexts (e.g., Indonesia) are particularly keen to make use of such tools. For my part, I discourage the use of such tools for those who work in institutions: 'free' tools are often tied to commercial interests, may compromise institutional policies to do with student privacy or enrolment, and are difficult to monitor. I point out, too, that the field of CALL is often plagued with the well-meaning tool development and use by a dynamic individual that fails to be sustained from one semester to another, or from one institution to another (Gruba & Hinkelman, 2012).

Despite pushing for the use of the LMS, I often lose the argument. One issue in using the LMS site is that students do not see it as relevant, or that it is not available within their low-resource institutions. If I mention that Moodle (an open-source LMS facility) is available for free installation [moodle.org], students note that they do not have the resources or ability to set up a shared server. Additionally, they argue that as junior or part-time academic faculty, they lack the political skills to be able to get the resources to put such a server in place. Despite such resistance, however, I push ahead in my efforts to teach the LMS: I think such training provides insights into the political realities of a large institution and allows students to see how full-time educational technology specialists create and manage a site. Using an LMS, too, helps keep us on track in achieving the *TESOL Technology Standards* for integrated delivery of assessments and student records.

In explaining my own location in the field, one requirement of the final papers is that students locate themselves to answer the question: Where is the project located in the landscape of educational technology? Without a clear position, I argue, students are vulnerable to writing mere descriptions of their work and so it fails to meet the goal that success in graduate school means a clear demonstration of critical thinking skills.

Students are asked to consider submitting their final assignments to conferences that focus on educational technologies; in an ever-more competitive marketplace for academic teaching positions, I am keen to see that my students have publications to back up their applications for work. In Australia, however, we do not have a professional organization that holds an annual event or conference specifically for computer-assisted language learning; accordingly, I ask students to submit their work to the highly regarded Australasian Society for

Computers in Learning in Tertiary Education [ascilite.org] that encompasses work to do with educational technology and design across for the region. Over the years, my graduate students have been successful in making presentations at conferences (e.g., Clark & Gruba, 2010) that have helped them in their early careers. Past students, too, have returned to give guest lectures about their own success in educational design companies, or starting up a business that provides online ESL materials to overseas colleges and universities.

Future directions

In the coming year, I intend to adopt the book *Teaching as a design science* (Laurillard, 2012) to underpin current materials and assigned reading. As with mainstream educational technology efforts, the book helps to strengthen the message that we each must make our efforts transparent and sustainable. Here, Laurillard sets out ways to establish a series of design patterns that I think can, and should, be adopted for use by CALL practitioners.

Further, in the coming years, we will all need to keep an eye on the prediction of Bax (2003) that technologies will indeed 'disappear' into the language curriculum. Mindful of this prediction, the material that I teach is meant to be adopted for use in other courses as a way to further integrate technologies into curriculum design, programme evaluation, research methods and language testing for example. With that dispersion of the role of technologies across applied linguistics, and the goal of CALL to be fully integrated (Garrision, 2009), the course will need to better situate the role of new media and new literacies in an era of global communication. Rather than highlight technologies, for example, such a course would see technologies as indeed normalised and then examine the changing roles of language through the study of areas such as identity performance (e.g., Zappavigna, 2014), metrolingualism (e.g., Pennycook & Otsuji, 2015), multimodal discourse analysis (e.g., O'Halloran, Marissa, Podlasov, & Tan, 2013), social semiotics (e.g., Kress, 2012; van Leeuwen, 2005) and the ethics of online intercultural research (e.g., Phipps, 2013). I continue to emphasize assessment and evaluation practices (Gruba et al., 2016). The course, I hope, helps students to enhance their critical thinking skills in ways they help them to navigate the fast-paced 'dynamic complex' (Garrett, 2009) that characterises the changing role of technologies throughout modern language programmes.

References

Bax, S. (2003). CALL – past, present and future. *System*, *31*, 13–28.

Blackboard (2015). Software facility. Retrieved from http://www.blackboard.com

Blommaert, J. (2010). *The sociolinguistics of globalization*. Cambridge: Cambridge University Press.

Burston, J. (2015). Twenty years of MALL project implementation: A meta-analysis of learning outcomes. *ReCALL*, *27*(01), 4–20.

Chambers, A., & Bax, S. (2006). Making CALL work: Towards normalisation. *System*, *34*, 465–479.

Chapelle, C. A. (1997). CALL in the year 2000: Still in search of research paradigms? *Language Learning & Technology*, *1*(1), 19–43.

Chapelle, C. A. (2001). *Computer applications in second language acquisition: Foundations for teaching, testing and research*. Cambridge: Cambridge University Press.

Chapelle, C. A. (2007). Challenges in the evaluation of innovation: Observations from technology research. *Innovation in Language Learning & Teaching*, *1*(1), 30–45.

Chapelle, C. A. (2014, August). Arguments for technology and language learning (video). Keynote speech at EuroCALL, 2104, University of Groningnen, Netherlands. Retrieved from https://www.eurocall2014.nl/

Clark, C., & Gruba, P. (2010). The use of social networking sites for foreign language learning: An autoethnographic study of LiveMocha. In C. H. Steel, M. J. Keppel, P. Gerbric, & S. Housego (Eds.), *Curriculum, technology & transformation for an unknown future*. Proceedings of ascilite Sydney 2010 (pp. 164–173). Retrieved from http://www.ascilite.org.au/conferences/sydney10/procs/Cclark-full.pdf

Cornillie, F., Thorne, S., & Desmet, P. (2012). *ReCALL* special issue: Digital games for language learning: Challenges and opportunities. *ReCALL*, *24*, 243–256.

Garrett, N. (2009). Computer-assisted language learning trends and issues revisited: Integrating innovation. *The Modern Language Journal*, *93*, 719–740.

Gibbes, M., & Carson, L. (2014). Project-based language learning: An activity theory analysis. *Innovation in Language Learning & Teaching*, *8*(2), 171–189.

Golonka, E. M., et al. (2012). Technologies for foreign language learning: A review of technology types and their effectiveness. *Computer Assisted Language Learning*, *27*(1), 70–105.

Grgurovic, M., & Hegelheimer, V. (2007). Help options and multimedia listening: Students' use of subtitles and the transcript. *Language Learning & Technology*, *11*(1), 45–66.

Gruba, P. (2006). Playing the videotext: A media literacy perspective on video-mediated L2 listening. *Language Learning & Technology*, *10*(2), 77–92.

Gruba, P., Cardenás-Claros, M., Suvorov, R., & Rick, K. (2016). *Blended language program evaluation*. Basingstoke, UK: Palgrave Macmillan.

Gruba, P., & Hinkelman, D. (2012). *Blending technologies in the second language classroom*. Basingstoke, UK: Palgrave Macmillan.

Healey, D., Hegelheimer, V., Hubbard, P., Ioannou-Georgiou, S., Kessler, G., & Ware, P. (2008). *TESOL Technology standards framework*. Alexandria, VA: TESOL.

Hulme, A. (2009). Will mobile learning change language learning? *ReCALL, 21*(02), 157–165.

Jauregi, K., Canto, S., de Graaff, R., Koenraad, T., & Moonen, M. (2011). Verbal interaction in Second Life: Towards a pedagogic framework for task design. *Computer Assisted Language Learning, 24*(1), 77–101.

Jones, R. H. H., & Hafner, C. A. A. (2012). *Understanding digital literacies*. Hoboken: Taylor and Francis.

Kramsch, C. (2014). Teaching foreign languages in an era of globalization: Introduction. *Modern Language Journal, 98*(1), 296–311.

Kress, G. (2009). Assessment in the perspective of a social semiotic theory of multimodal teaching and learning. In C. Wyatt-Smith & J. J. Cumming (Eds.), *Educational assessment in the 21st century: Connecting theory and practice* (pp. 19–41). New York: Springer.

Kress, G. (2012). Thinking about the notion of 'cross-cultural' from a social semiotic perspective. *Language & Intercultural Communication, 12*(4), 369–385.

Kress, G. R., & van Leeuwen, T. (2006). *Reading images: The grammar of visual design* (2nd ed.). New York: Routledge.

Laurillard, D. (2012). *Teaching as design science*. New York, London: Routledge.

Licoppe, C., & Morel, J. (2012). Video-in-interaction: 'Talking heads' and the multimodal organization of mobile and Skype video calls. *Research on Language and Social Interaction, 45*(4), 399–429. doi: 10.1080/08351813.2012.724996

Lotherington, H., & Jenson, J. (2011). Teaching multimodal and digital literacy in second language settings: New literacies, new basics, new pedagogies. *Annual Review of Applied Linguistics, 31*, 226–248.

Lund, A. (2008). Wikis: A collective approach to language production. *ReCALL, 20*(1), 35–54.

O'Halloran, K. L., Marissa, K. L. E., Podlasov, A., & Tan, S. (2013). Multimodal digital semiotics: The interaction of language with other resources. *Text & Talk, 33*(4–5), 665–690.

Pennycook, A., & Otsuji, E. (2015). *Metrolingualism: Language in the city*. New York: Taylor and Francis.

Pennycook, A. (2008). Critical applied linguistics and language education. In S. May and N. Hornberger (Eds.), *Enclyclopedia of Language and Education* (pp. 169–182). New York: Springer.

Phipps, A. (2013). Intercultural ethics: Questions of methods in language and intercultural communication. *Language & Intercultural Communication, 13*(1), 10–26.

van Leeuwen, T. (2005). *Introducing social semiotics*. New York: Routledge.

Vandergrift, L. (2007). Recent developments in second and foreign language listening comprehension research. *Language Teaching*, 40(3), 191–210.

Wagner, E. (2010). The effect of the use of video texts on ESL listening test-taker performance. *Language Testing, 27*(4), 493–513.

Wang, S. & Smith, S. (2013). Reading and grammar learning through mobile phones. *Language Learning & Technology, 17*(3), 117–134.

Waters, A. (2009). Managing innovation in English language education. *Language Teaching, 42*(04), 421–458.

Zappavigna, M. (2014). Enacting identity in microblogging through ambient affiliation. *Discourse & Communication, 8*(2), 209–228.

4

CALL Research, Practice and Teachers' Roles

Jeong-Bae Son
University of Southern Queensland, Australia

Introduction

Computer-assisted language learning (CALL) involves the use of computers and digital technologies for language learning. In the form of formal professional development for language teachers, a CALL training course is normally offered as part of Applied Linguistics and/or TESOL (Teaching English to Speakers of Other Languages) programmes at universities. The CALL course at the University of Southern Queensland (USQ) has been offered by distance education, online and on-campus for over fifteen years and has trained over 1,200 postgraduate students (predominantly distance and online students) from over twenty countries. Since the author wrote the original course material in 2000 (Son, 2000), the course has been continuously updated in various ways while keeping the same foundation. This chapter describes the underlying approach taken in the course and the content of the course. It also looks at features of the course and discusses issues and challenges of teaching the course. It concludes with future directions for the further development of the course.

Context

LIN8006 Computer-Assisted Language Learning is one of the elective courses that can be taken as part of the Master of Education (Applied Linguistics) or Master of Education (TESOL) programme offered through the School of Linguistics, Adult and Specialist Education at USQ. The degree programme requires one and a half years full-time or part-time equivalent study and students are typically required to take a total of twelve units (courses) to complete the programme. Core courses of the Master's programme normally include: 'The Nature of Language'; 'Principles of Second Language Learning'; and 'Methodology in Teaching a Second Language'. Other elective courses include: 'Computer-Assisted Language Learning'; 'Introduction to Sociolinguistics'; 'Language and Literacy Assessment'; 'Discourse Analysis' and 'Language Program Management'. The CALL course can be also taken as a Professional Development Single Course.

The University's teaching year is divided into three semesters and each semester has at least twelve weeks of teaching. Among the three semesters, the CALL course is currently offered online in Semester 1 (from March to June) and Semester 2 (from mid-July to October) and on campus (subject to the number of enrolments) in Semester 1. Students can take the CALL course in the semester of their choice while they are recommended to take the CALL course after they complete the 'Nature of Language', 'Principles of Second Language Learning' and/or 'Methodology in Teaching a Second Language' courses. They are expected to complete all their learning and assessment for the CALL course within a semester. Since 2008, all USQ courses, including the CALL course, have been delivered through Moodle, an open source learning management system (LMS), which provides students with course information, materials, forums and resources. Regardless of their enrolment mode (online or on-campus), all students are given access to the online learning platform.

Course description

The CALL course is an introduction to the theory and practice of CALL. This intention is reflected in the following rationale for the course that has remained the same despite the fact that numerous changes have been made to the course content over the years:

> With the advance of computer technology and the growth of interest in the use of computers for education, it is necessary for language teachers to become aware of the application of computers in second/foreign language learning and teaching. In other words, language teachers need to know about the basics of Computer-Assisted Language Learning (CALL) in order not to be left behind in the use of instructional technology for enhancing learning and teaching.

Specifically, the course is designed to introduce postgraduate students (mainly, in-service teachers) to the field of CALL by providing them with insights into key aspects of CALL and the basic knowledge of the practical use of CALL applications and tools in language education. It takes a modular approach and consists of three main modules: (1) background; (2) research; and (3) language teachers in CALL environments (for a course overview, see Appendix A). The idea of having the three modules was originally based on two fundamental questions the author had in mind when he developed the course: 'What do language teachers need to know about CALL?' and 'What can language teachers do with CALL?' These questions could be considered as a guide to explore what CALL is and how language teachers can use CALL while developing their knowledge and skills for CALL practice.

Given the three modules, the CALL course begins with a discussion on basic concepts of CALL, while identifying terms associated with CALL. The second module reviews previous research on CALL and looks at trends and issues in CALL research. The final module discusses language teachers' roles and tasks in CALL environments in terms of observation, design, implementation, evaluation and management. Thus, course topics include theoretical bases for CALL; research directions in CALL; language teachers' roles in CALL; the design and evaluation of CALL applications such as multimedia/hypermedia materials, websites and online tools; and strategies for integrating CALL into second/foreign language programmes.

Each module contains its own learning objectives, readings and learning activities. There is no prescribed text for the course. Instead, a number of selected readings (journal articles and book chapters) accessible through the USQ Library are recommended for the learning activities, which give students the opportunity to actively engage with the course content. Table 4.1 shows a sample list of the course readings for Semesters 1 and 2 in 2016. Starting from those basic readings that are updated when needed, students are encouraged to search for more references and share them with other fellow students.

In Module 2, specifically, students are given opportunities to explore CALL research topics and themes that are widely discussed and studied in the field of CALL. The topics and themes include: research (e.g., theories, approaches, methods); pedagogy (e.g., methodology, implementation, instruction, practice, activities, tasks, blended learning, feedback, integration, interaction); technology (e.g., hardware, software, tools, systems, platforms, learning environments, e-portfolios, databases, blogs, wikis, digital tools, resources); learners (e.g., students, learning styles, learner training, learner attitudes, perceptions); teachers (e.g., lecturers, teaching styles, teacher training, teacher attitudes, perceptions, professional development); design (e.g., software development, website interface, app design); evaluation (e.g., courseware evaluation, website evaluation, app reviews); reading;

Table 4.1 Topics and selected readings for each module of the CALL course in 2016

Topics	Selected Readings
Module 1: Background (Weeks 1–2)	
1.1 Points of departure 1.2 Past, present and future of CALL 1.3 CALL environments	Bax (2011); Blake (2011); Davies, Otto, & Ruschoff (2012); Stockwell & Tanaka-Ellis (2012)
Module 2: Research (Weeks 3–4)	
2.1 Trends and issues 2.2 Agendas for CALL studies 2.3 Research topics and themes	Chun (2012); Garrett (2009); Grgurović, Chapelle, & Shelley (2013)
Module 3: Language Teachers in CALL Environments (Weeks 5–15)	
3.1 Observation: The learner; the teacher and the computer	Hubbard (2013); Son, Robb, & Charismiadji (2011)
3.2 Design: CALL software design; CALL authoring; activity design	Hampel & Pleines (2013); Otto & Pusack (2009); Son (2007)
3.3 Implementation: Planning CALL lessons; using CALL materials and activities	Chapelle & Jamieson (2008); Stanley (2013)
3.4 Evaluation: Evaluation components; evaluation instruments	Son (2005); Son & Park (2012)
3.5 Management: Organizing a CALL lab; managing CALL resources	MacDonald (2011); Son (2011)

listening; writing; speaking; vocabulary (e.g., dictionaries, glosses); grammar; pronunciation; culture; testing (e.g., language assessment, computer adaptive testing, computer-based tests); concordancing (e.g., corpora, concordancers); gaming (e.g., digital games, mobile games); computer-mediated communication (CMC) (e.g., telecollaboration, videoconferencing); web-based language learning (WBLL) (e.g., language learning websites, web resources); mobile-assisted language learning (MALL); robot-assisted language learning (RALL); and intelligent computer-assisted language learning (ICALL) (Son, 2014c, 2015).

In order to pass the course, students are required to successfully complete two assessment items: Assignment 1 (due in the middle of the semester) and Assignment 2 (due at the end of the semester). Each assignment consists of two parts (Part A and Part B) and assignment tasks include a literature review, discussion forums and an evaluation report. In each semester, different topics of the literature review and different CALL materials for the evaluation report are chosen and advised by the course examiner in relation to the course readings, activities and resources of interest. For the discussion forums, on the other hand, students are required to make postings to designated course discussion areas regularly in line with the given learning activities. Throughout the semester, they are expected to submit their own responses to each learning activity containing a certain task or open-ended questions. All assignments are assessed according to the criteria that will be elaborated in the next section.

Features and issues

Role-based approach

A distinctive feature of the CALL course is its focus on the teacher's roles in CALL environments. The course suggests that the teacher can be a CALL observer, designer, implementer, evaluator or manager, in addition to a tutor, guide or facilitator in the language classroom. The sub-headings of the third module of the course reflect those things the teacher can do (i.e., observation, design, implementation, evaluation and management), rather than activities (e.g., using concordance programmes, using web activities, using mobile apps) or tools (e.g., communication tools, presentation tools, resource sharing tools). By taking this approach, the course encourages students to actively respond to the need for finding appropriate roles to engage with CALL (Son, 2000).

As with other introductory courses, the course does not cover all aspects of the subject in depth. While it attempts to explore the field of CALL broadly, its coverage is somehow limited by the choice of components within a single course. When there is a need to change the main body of the course, it would be possible to take a different approach to present the course content. If a skill-based approach is chosen, for example, the following topic areas might be considered: reading; writing; listening; speaking; pronunciation; vocabulary; grammar; culture; concordancing; testing; gaming; CMC; WBLL; and MALL. Whichever approach is taken, it is important to update the contents constantly in order to keep up with advancements in pedagogy and technology. Due to the nature of CALL, the expectation to keep the state-of-the-art status is higher in a CALL course than in any other applied linguistics courses.

Task-based contextual learning

The sequence of learning is aligned with learning activities that require students to read the selected readings, link with their teaching situations and do meaningful tasks with open-ended questions related to the thought-provoking topics of each module. In Learning Activity 3.5, for example, students are guided to read Hampel and Pleines (2013) and respond to the following task with pedagogical considerations: 'This reading focuses on activity design in a Moodle-based virtual learning environment (VLE). How do you see the importance of research examining student engagement and interaction in the design of online activities? What recommendation would you make based on the study reported in the reading? Post your responses to the discussion board.' Similarly, in Learning Activity 3.11, students read Son (2005) and respond to another task based on the reading: 'The checklist offered in this reading has fifteen general evaluation criteria for evaluating language learning websites. Which criterion do you think is the most important one? Why? Can you think of other criteria that may affect your judgement of the quality of a certain website? Post your responses to the discussion board.' In a nutshell, they are invited to read a research paper and participate in discussions on the main topic of the research paper to complete a contextual task.

Each week enrolled students are required to read at least 1–2 selected papers on the given topics. However, there is an uncertainty in the amount of their reading and study time even though they are encouraged to search for and read more recent and relevant papers in constructivist learning environments. Thus, there is a need to address the question of how the course can continuously motivate them to learn more about the topics and get actively involved in the discussion forums. Another issue is that there is the difficulty of providing hands-on practice to online students who are not physically present at the same time and the same place. While all students are given opportunities to ask any CALL-related questions at any time and participate in CMC activities such as asynchronous discussion forums and synchronous online meetings through Blackboard Collaborate (http://www.blackboard.com/online-collaborative-learning/) or Zoom (https://zoom.us/), little hands-on techniques and skills to use certain hardware, software or tools are offered to online students. In line with these issues, CALL training programmes are called for to guide teachers to develop self-directed and collaborative learning strategies for autonomous professional development in CALL (Son, 2014b; Son, Robb, Hubbard, Stevens, & Seburn, 2015) so that the teachers can find ways of acquiring and improving their technical skills themselves.

Interaction and collaboration

There is a strong emphasis on the importance of students' contribution to online discussion forums. Students are expected to make postings to LMS-based course discussion areas regularly according to the suggested study schedule. All students are allowed to see and compare each other's postings and comment on the postings. They are recommended to participate in various types of discussions on CALL for interaction and collaboration with other participants. With the aim to generate constructive discussions on CALL research and practice, this online activity provides them with practical experience of CMC and communication channels for sharing thoughts, ideas and resources with their fellow students. The course examiner (lecturer) observes, facilitates and moderates the discussions as needed.

Through investigations of patterns of interactions generated in online discussion groups of the CALL course, six message types were identified in Son's (2002, 2006) studies: task-based messages; interactive messages; self-introductory messages from the students; informative messages from the lecturer; erroneous/repeated messages; messages related to administrative matters. Among them, task-based messages and interactive messages were the most common message types (totalling over 87% of all postings). In the interactive messages, another six types of student-student interactions were also identified: giving opinions/ideas; expressing support; asking questions; providing information; offering thanks; and greetings. It was found that there was a moderate to high degree of peer support and collaboration. Participants' time, personal interest and working knowledge were the most noticeable factors that affected the degree of interaction and collaboration. It should be meaningful to continue to examine the relationship between the level of interaction in online discussions and the level of achievement in CALL courses offered in a variety of platforms.

Criteria-based assessment

As mentioned earlier, course assessment items include a literature review, discussion forums and an evaluation report. Each assignment is assessed using a distinctive marking rubric containing detailed criteria: criteria for marking the literature review are the 'selection and coverage of the literature', 'critical analysis of the literature', 'originality and creativity of the review' and 'overall presentation and referencing conventions'; criteria for marking the discussion forums are the 'overview and control of the task', 'knowledge and understanding of the topic in the question', 'quality of analysis' and 'overall presentation and referencing conventions' (see Appendix B for a sample marking rubric); and criteria for marking the evaluation report are the 'description of the selected website or app', 'quality of analysis', '"integration of the website or app" and "overview and overall presentation". Essentially, critical thinking and analysis skills are considered as crucial in the assessment.

While the marking rubrics offer a systematic approach to the course assessment (Montgomery, 2002) and grades are awarded based on the achievement level of performance standards stated in the assessment criteria (Sadler, 2005), the assessment might be potentially too prescriptive, thereby limiting the value of creativity (Beghetto, 2005). To address this issue, assessment tasks need to be chosen to assess the learning outcomes appropriately and enable students to construct and develop their understanding and knowledge of the selected topics and their ideas of responding intelligently to the assignment requirements. The question of how much assignments can cover the course content also needs to be considered and reviewed regularly in line with the amount of student learning that can be accommodated in a single course. In addition, marking reliability needs to be evaluated and improved whenever possible to represent the level of academic quality accurately and meaningfully.

Future directions

The CALL course started as one of the elective courses for the postgraduate programmes in Applied Linguistics and TESOL at USQ. It is not certain how long the current programme structure will be maintained as the offering of the course can be affected by organizational decisions and priorities. Within the programmes, for example, there was another technology-related course titled 'Internet-Based Language Instruction' (IBLI) offered from 2004 to 2008. The IBLI course was removed from the Applied Linguistics and TESOL programmes in 2009 through the restructuring of the programmes. The CALL course was a prerequisite for the IBLI course. For those students who completed the introductory CALL course, the IBLI course allowed them to study more about CALL with a focus on both the theory and practice of IBLI. Topics of the IBLI course included basics of the Internet, locating and using Internet-based resources and communication tools for language instruction, issues associated with the use of the Internet in second/foreign language learning and teaching and the creation of web-based language learning environments. The IBLI course combined guided modules and online discussions with investigatory components leading to the submission of a web-based portfolio containing five basic pages: a homepage (showing a self-introduction and a table of contents); a research page (presenting a review of the current literature on one aspect of the use of the Internet for language teaching); a teaching page (presenting an IBLI lesson plan); a resources page (presenting an annotated list of WBLL activities/tasks and an annotated list of websites for language teacher development);

and a reflection page (presenting a reflective journal) (Son, 2004, 2009). If an opportunity to develop and offer another new CALL-related course arises, a conscientious effort will need to be made to explore new pedagogical practices with emerging technologies.

The CALL course helps language teachers (postgraduate students) develop basic competencies in CALL. In a study on the transfer of CALL coursework to classroom practice, Son (2014a) reported that the large majority of teachers who had completed the CALL course agreed that the CALL course positively influenced their use of computers for teaching purposes and highly valued the CALL knowledge and skills they had gained from the CALL course. The current version of the course will be constantly updated in future semesters. The update is likely to reflect the increasing importance of digital language teaching covering digital literacy, mobile learning, social networking, digital storytelling, digital games and open educational resources. It will provide students with more guidance on the effective use of digital tools and focus more on supporting the students' personal learning strategies for autonomous professional development in CALL. By being self-directed learners in online environments, the students will be confident in meeting the challenges of the future.

References

Bax, S. (2011). Normalisation revisited: The effective use of technology in language education. *International Journal of Computer-Assisted Language Learning and Teaching, 1*(2), 1–15.

Beghetto, R. A. (2005). Does assessment kill student creativity? *The Educational Forum, 69*(3), 254–263.

Blake, R. J. (2011). Current trends in online language learning. *Annual Review of Applied Linguistics, 31*, 19–35.

Chapelle, C. A., & Jamieson, J. (2008). *Tips for teaching with CALL: Practical approaches to computer-assisted language learning*. White Plains, NY: Pearson Education.

Chun, D. M. (2012). Replication studies in CALL research. *CALICO Journal, 29*(4), 591–600.

Davies, G., Otto, S. E. K., & Ruschoff, B. (2012). Historical perspectives on CALL. In M. Thomas, H. Reinders & M. Warschauer (Eds.), *Contemporary computer-assisted language learning* (pp. 19–38). London: Bloomsbury Academic.

Garrett, N. (2009). Computer-assisted language learning trends and issues revisited: Integrating innovation. *The Modern Language Journal, 93*(Winter), 719–740.

Grgurović, M., Chapelle, C. A., & Shelley, M. C. (2013). A meta-analysis of effectiveness studies on computer technology-supported language learning. *ReCALL, 25*(2), 165–198.

Hampel, R., & Pleines, C. (2013). Fostering student interaction and engagement in a virtual learning environment: An investigation into activity design and implementation. *CALICO Journal*, *30*(3), 342–370.

Hubbard, P. (2013). Making a case for learner training in technology enhanced language learning environments. *CALICO Journal*, *30*(2), 163–178.

MacDonald, L. (2011). The virtual language lab: Virtually painless simply real. *The IALLT Journal for Language Learning Technologies*, *41*(1), 137–160. Retrieved from http://www.iallt.org/iallt_journal/the_virtual_language_lab_virtually_painless_simply_real

Montgomery, K. (2002). Authentic tasks and rubrics: Going beyond traditional assessments in college teaching. *College Teaching*, *50*(1), 34–39.

Otto, S. E. K., & Pusack, J. P. (2009). Computer-assisted language learning authoring issues. *The Modern Language Journal*, *93*(Winter), 784–801.

Sadler, D. R. (2005). Interpretations of criteria-based assessment and grading in higher education. *Assessment and Evaluation in Higher Education*, *30*(2), 175–194.

Son, J.-B. (2000). *Computer-assisted language learning: Study book*. Toowoomba, Australia: University of Southern Queensland.

Son, J.-B. (2002). Online discussion in a CALL course for distance language teachers. *CALICO Journal*, *20*, 127–144.

Son, J.-B. (2004). *Internet-based language instruction: Study book*. Toowoomba, Australia: University of Southern Queensland.

Son, J.-B. (2005). Exploring and evaluating language learning web sites. In J.-B. Son, & S. O'Neill (Eds.), *Enhancing learning and teaching: Pedagogy, technology and language* (pp. 215–227). Flaxton, Australia: Post Pressed.

Son, J.-B. (2006). Using online discussion groups in a CALL teacher training course. *RELC Journal*, *37*, 123–135.

Son, J.-B. (2007). Learner experiences in web-based language learning. *Computer Assisted Language Learning*, *20*(1), 21–36.

Son, J.-B. (2009). Using Web-based portfolios in CALL teacher education. In J.-B. Son (Ed.), *Internet-based language learning: Pedagogies and technologies* (pp. 107–118). APACALL Book Series Volume 2. Raleigh, NC: Lulu.

Son, J.-B. (2011). Online tools for language teaching. *TESL-EJ*, *15*(1). Retrieved from http://www.tesl-ej.org/wordpress/issues/volume15/ej57/ej57int/

Son, J.-B. (2014a). Moving beyond basics: From CALL coursework to classroom practice and professional development. In J.-B. Son (Ed.), *Computer-assisted language learning: Learners, teachers and tools* (pp. 122–149). APACALL Book Series Volume 3. Newcastle upon Tyne, UK: Cambridge Scholars Publishing.

Son, J.-B. (2014b). Learning about computer-assisted language learning: Online tools and professional development. In J.-B. Son (Ed.), *Computer-assisted language learning: Learners, teachers and tools* (pp. 173–186). APACALL Book Series Volume 3. Newcastle upon Tyne, UK: Cambridge Scholars Publishing.

Son, J.-B. (2014c, November). CALL research and practice: Where are we up to? Keynote speech at the Asia Association of Computer Assisted Language Learning (AsiaCALL) 2014 Conference, National Changhua University of Education, Changhua, Taiwan.

Son, J.-B. (2015, November). Computer-assisted language learning: A reality check. Plenary speech at the Globalization and Localization in CALL (GLoCALL) 2015 Conference, Pai Chai University, Daejeon, Korea.
Son, J.-B., & Park, J.-Y. (2012). Intercultural usability of language learning websites. *International Journal of Pedagogies and Learning, 7*(2), 135–141.
Son, J.-B., Robb, T., & Charismiadji, I. (2011). Computer literacy and competency: A survey of Indonesian teachers of English as a foreign language. *CALL-EJ, 12*(1), 26–42. Retrieved from http://callej.org/journal/12-1/Son_2011.pdf
Son, J.-B., Robb, T., Hubbard, P., Stevens, V., & Seburn, T. (2015, March). Self-directed professional development in computer-assisted language learning. Colloquium conducted at the TESOL 2015 International Convention & English Language Expo, Metro Toronto Convention Centre, Toronto, Canada. Retrieved from http://www.apacall.org/member/sonjb/speeches/tesol2015/Son_etal_4Es_TESOL2015.pdf
Stanley, G. (2013). *Language learning with technology: Ideas for integrating technology in the classroom*. Cambridge: Cambridge University Press.
Stockwell, G., & Tanaka-Ellis, N. (2012). Diversity in environments. In G. Stockwell (Ed.), *Computer-assisted language learning: Diversity in research and practice* (pp. 71–89). Cambridge: Cambridge University Press.

Appendix A

CALL course overview

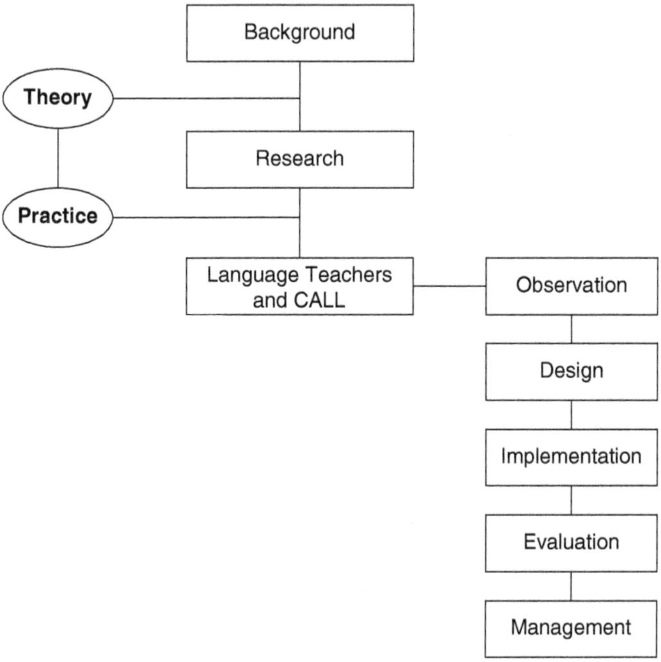

Appendix B

Sample Marking Rubric for Discussion Forums

	F (<50%)	C (50–64.9%)	B (65–74.9%)	A (75–84.9%)	HD (>85%)
1. Overview and control of the task (15%)					
Perspective provided; length suitable to topic; materials suitable to topic; required number of postings	Demonstrates faulty or inappropriate overview and control of the task	Demonstrates limited overview and control of the task; limited responses	Demonstrates adequate overview and control of the task; adequate responses	Demonstrates very good overview and control of the task; very good responses	Demonstrates excellent overview and control of the task; excellent responses
2. Knowledge and understanding of the topic in the question (25%)					
Reliable information; thoroughness; grasp of issues; wide reading	Demonstrates serious deficiencies in understanding and applying fundamental concepts; presents undeveloped or inappropriate information or arguments	Demonstrates limited knowledge and understanding of the topic	Demonstrates adequate knowledge and understanding of the topic	Demonstrates very clear and relevant knowledge and understanding of the topic	Demonstrates high quality knowledge and understanding of the topic
3. Quality of analysis (40%)					
Authors' positions stated clearly; salient points directly addressed; logical development; insights offered	Poorly written and analysed; inappropriate content	Limited level of analysis; limited for this level of study; some inadequacies	Adequate level of analysis; adequate for this level of study; soundly developed	Substantial level of analysis; substantial for this level of study; clearly articulated and capably developed	High quality level of analysis; excellent for this level of study; very clearly articulated and very skilfully developed
4. Overall presentation and referencing conventions (20%)					
APA conventions; logical structure; grammar, spelling, punctuation and style; within the word limit	Fails to demonstrate the basis requirements of the assignment; inappropriate for an academic assignment; inaccuracies cause severe weaknesses in some or all conventions of writing and presentation	Weaknesses in referencing conventions; inconsistencies and/or inaccuracies cause concern	Conventions of writing and presentation reasonably attended to; some inaccuracies	Most conventions are well attended to; very few inconsistencies and/or inaccuracies	High quality presentation; all conventions are well attended to; error free

5

Language Learning and Technology

A Thirty-Year Journey

Gary Motteram
University of Manchester, UK

Introduction

We have seen a steady growth in the use of digital technologies in society and there is an increasing availability of technology for teachers to use in many institutions in many parts of the world. This is particularly true in higher education, but is increasingly the case in secondary and primary schools in the developed world and parts of the developing world. We have also seen a growing interest in technology-enhanced language learning and courses that work to develop teachers' skills, both in pre- and in-service education and research into these topics (Guichon & Hauck, 2011). This chapter reports on one of what I would argue is the longest running of such courses (module in the United Kingdom) in the world, perhaps the first, and while the content of the course has changed and developed, it still has a connection to its earliest first running version in 1986.

Context

The University of Manchester in the United Kingdom has been running courses designed specifically for English language teachers since 1962 and has been actively working with teachers exploring the role that technology can play in supporting language development since the mid-1980s. We started in an era when classroom computers in the United Kingdom were the BBC Micro, were stand alone, and when none of the teachers we worked with had any experiences of using them either for personal or professional reasons. We now find ourselves in a very different world technologically where in many contexts both teachers and learners are able to bring their own devices (BYOD) and the institution's technological contribution, if any, might be very good access to fast Wi-Fi. Students are now, mostly, tech savvy; they are increasingly net natives, born and raised in a world where digital technologies have always been there. They bring a range of high-tech devices to class: laptops, mobile phones and tablets. As time goes on, some will no doubt have a Pebble, or an Apple watch, or bring other emerging technologies to the class. The question that this chapter addresses, therefore, is if the students have good access to new technologies and appear to know how to use them, what should a course like this one cover?

Course description

In this chapter, I focus on the core course that all of our students on our MA TESOL and those who take the TESOL pathway on the MA in Digital Technologies Communication and Education are expected to follow. This course unit is now called Language Learning and Technology. In earlier incarnations this course unit was called Educational Technology for English Language Teaching and the shift in name reflects the changing emphasis of the course. Early versions of the course unit did focus much more on technology per se and we would spend time showing people how the devices turned on, how to load and run software, actions like formatting a floppy disk and so on. We spent a lot of time training people, and I use the term training here deliberately, to use technologies and then consider their role in language learning. The current course unit takes a much more language learning driven approach, mainly because we do not have to spend as much time on the technology. However, having said that, I have recently introduced a practical tutorial as a response to student feedback, where we do focus on specific software and develop skills and techniques. This is not currently a compulsory part of the course and students are not obliged to attend.

The Language Learning and Technology course is offered both as a face-to-face course and as part of our distance provision. Both versions of the course are what might be termed blended. Both the face-to-face class and the online course, taught in Blackboard (Manchester's local virtual learning environment (VLE)), make use of a core set of online materials that have been created in Wikispaces as an open educational resource. You can see the materials at http://7006--llt.wikispaces.com. While these materials are open for anyone to view and could be used as the basis of other courses, they do make reference to the Manchester course, there are some links back to Blackboard, for example. It is, however, my intention to work to make these materials free standing and Manchester independent.

The course covers a number of different topics that are a mixture of skills and activity focus. We explore reading, writing and speaking overtly, with listening subsumed in an exploration of video in language learning, although video also includes a discussion of learners creating video and video conferencing. We look at text manipulation and concordancing, and we consider computer mediated communication, digital games, task-based learning and project work and taking an integrated approach.

The course unit starts by setting the scene and works through an activity in class that is reflected on. This is linked to the tutor-tool debate first brought into the field of technology in language learning by Levy (1997), but still a useful dichotomy today. The argument made is that we should be looking at software that we use in learning in terms of the functions it has. The distinction is usually made between software that teaches and software that is a generic tool that is made use of by the teacher for the needs of the lesson. The lesson that I present uses a spreadsheet and the objective is to elicit background information about the students' uses of technology in their classrooms (some of the data collected is discussed later in the chapter). Methodologically, the lesson is what Woodward (1986, 2003) would describe as 'loop input'. The task replicates a lesson that you might use in a language classroom, but uses content that relates directly to language teaching and technology. We go through a learning sequence in class and at the same time I collect information about the current student group. This allows us to open up the debate on how teachers might approach the use of technology in the classroom and it enables us to begin to develop a shared discourse. There is still an assumption for many software developers that the main role of technology is that of a 'tutor', in many cases for independent learning, and we find this in many of the apps that are developed for smartphones, for example, where we are engaging in activities that help us learn vocabulary, or grammar (Sweeney & Moore, 2012). However a lot of teachers working in the field make use of tools that are not designed for language teaching. This has been made increasingly easier by the development of tools on the Internet, what Dudeney and Hockly (2012) refer to as the 'the great shift' (p. 536) and which are often referred to as Web 2.0 tools, or social media. Using this distinction gives the students the beginnings of a vocabulary that they can start to use to talk about their contexts and what they do and they also start to think about why they do certain activities in class.

The next phase of the course unit builds on this to start talking about digital literacy. The emphasis shifts to reading and the significant change in reading that took place with the development of the web. It also now looks at new developments in reading and the new devices that some people are using. However, we start with an older article by Burbules (1997) that raises interesting issues about the rhetorics of the web and how web pages are constructed, how links work, what they mean and how we might categorize them. The key point that he makes in the early part of the chapter is that 'reading is a practice':

> The act of reading on a computer screen is not the same as reading out of a book; the pragmatics of reading-the speed of our reading, when we pause, how long we can concentrate, how often we skip over material or jump back and reread what we have read before, and so forth-are clearly going to be different, and these differences affect how we interpret, understand, and remember what we read. (p. 102)

Whether we read a printed book, or a traditional newspaper, a newspaper online, a book or a magazine on a Kindle, a tablet, or a phone, our processing of the text changes. I choose to deliver the 'content' of this course unit via an online wiki. In the very early versions of the distance course unit, they were delivered as printed booklets, sent out in the post. With the wiki, I change my relationship with the material and with the students. Different students (and non-students) can access the material in different ways to suit their own needs and reading preferences. They can read online, download the text as a pdf and then look at it on their preferred reading software, for example, Adobe Reader, Kindle, more specialist tools like Mendeley, or they can print it out. They can read it in the quiet of their home, or on the way to work on public transport. If they want to, they can also contribute to the text by gaining editor rights to the wiki, although to be candid, it is usually me that adds ideas and suggestions from the students to the wiki which I pick up from discussion forums, or from contributions in class. The material on the wiki is not just text, it is multimedia with pictures, video, PowerPoints with spoken commentaries and also listening texts.

We can also then relate our reading of Burbules to standard ELT practices on teaching learners to read and discuss 'skimming' and 'scanning' and text decoding, the role of vocabulary knowledge in reading. We look at how these are changed by electronic texts which we know that many people do not read fully and where looking up a word in a dictionary or getting a translation is very easy. As part of this section we also explore webquests (Dodge, 1995), a technique for exploring the web in a managed way, but emphasising problem solving and critical engagement.

The students then engage in an initial group activity. This is a device to get them to explore wikis in more depth and at the same time to consider the topics of cognition and metacognition. For the distance students, this task can be quite challenging because meeting up across different times zones is difficult to organize. Together the students produce a short online presentation about the role that cognition and metacognition play in reading. Once the task is complete, they are encouraged to reflect on their experiences and this activity is recalled once they get on to looking at collaborative writing later in the course.

The next phase of the course focuses on exploring language initially through text reconstruction, but then through concordancing. Text reconstruction is a topic that has not been discussed in the literature as often in the recent past as it was in the early days of CALL. It is related to the world of tutorial CALL (Hubbard & Siskin, 2004), and has its theoretical underpinnings in the SLA literature on 'noticing' (Schmidt, 1990) and the output hypothesis (Swain, 2000). Handley (2012) is one article that explores task-based learning, the role of interactive whiteboards and text reconstruction. It was shown in this article, as had been shown in earlier studies that text reconstruction activities have a positive impact on fluency. What is important here is the pedagogy of the task. Handley demonstrates that for learners to get the best out of their limited language learning time in class, teachers need to be able to set up tasks that allow learners to engage with language that allows them to both discuss language and how it works, thus giving them the opportunity to 'notice' different elements.

Software for text reconstruction has remained stable and only on the web, not having made the transition into the world of apps. We do, however, see similar tools appearing that still allow teachers to author their own tasks, allowing them to give opportunities for students to explore and talk about language, if the tasks are set up effectively. It is about the way that the technologies are combined with other classroom practices that make them effective and we see more of this later.

Concordancing also allows us to explore language in a variety of different ways. The collection of corpora by major publishers and the use of concordancing software has had a major impact on the content of course books (Dudeney & Hockly, 2012). We have also seen the continued use of these tools by teachers in classrooms, although this is usually work with adults and is often connected to English for Academic Purposes (EAP) or English for Special Purposes (ESP). This is often referred to as Data Driven Learning, a term coined by Johns (1986). Corpora and concordancing are seen as tools to give us more insight into both grammar and also lexis. This can lead us into a discussion about the roles that lexis and collocation play in language development and it gives students both a resource for the design of classroom materials and a way of exploring their own understanding of language.

The next topic we cover is that of video in language learning. Video has become so pervasive in language materials and in the world that video is often used as a replacement for audio in listening practice and this is where we start our exploration in the course. However, we quickly broaden our scope to explore some of the topics that Vanderplank (2010) in a survey article highlighted as being important areas to focus on:

> language and cultural learning; the continuing fascination with captions and subtitles in both L2 and L1 development; incidental language learning from broadcast TV; the use of so-called advance organizers to help learners access programmes; the need to train learners in media literacy or strategies; developments in the technology itself; global and satellite broadcasting; and video in listening assessment. (p. 9)

We look at the practice of using video in class through early works like Willis (1983), who developed a comprehensive taxonomy of tasks, but we also look at recent developments which have made it possible for almost anyone to create videos that are explored in books like Goldstein and Driver (2015) who in Part 2 of their book explore learner made materials. Finally we turn to the use of video conferencing (see Devellotte, Guichon, & Vincent, 2010), but this is picked up later again when we cover computer-mediated communication (CMC).

Following on from video we consider writing. We look back at the early work in this area that links the developments of the process writing approach to word processing. This is most effectively summarized in Pennington (1996) where she suggests a cause-effect cycle in which we see writing events linked to a series of stages through which the writer will develop:

- writing easier
- writing more
- writing differently
- writing better (Pennington, 1996, p. 127)

We then explore the use of other tools in writing, email for example (Slaouti et al., 2000) and then the more recent uses of tools like wikis, which get the group talking about collaboration. There have been a number of studies that explore this topic including Storch (2005) and Kessler et al. (2012). We are also beginning to explore what impact mobile devices might have on learners' writing and the sorts of tools that might support these developments. In my own writing I have argued that these tools are Technical Cultural Artefacts, tools that are created for one use, but are appropriated by teachers for other uses (Motteram, 2013) and in some cases like with word processors the tools actually make a change of pedagogy possible. Another example of this is Skype (Motteram, 2013). Without the advent of the word processor it is unlikely that we would have seen the rapid growth of the process writing approach, or the intercultural exchanges discussed in O'Dowd (2013), or Devellotte, Guichon and Vincent (2010).

Writing links well into CMC, particularly through mobile technologies and the development of Web 2.0 where we find a significant development in the use of writing to communicate, in one of the ironies of the development of mobile phones. Whereas in the past when I asked what teachers and their learners wrote on a regular basis, I would get few responses beyond the needs of schooling and university. Some writing might continue in the workplace, but little occurred elsewhere. Texting changed all this and while we all walk around with mobile devices that are capable of making calls, we see a massive growth in the use of text in our world with, it is suggested, something like 300 billion messages sent in the United Kingdom in 2014 (Garside, 2014). The big growth in 2014 was reputed to have been because of the growth of mobile apps that encouraged such interactivity. CMC does not just refer to the use of text for communication, but also includes the multimodal video conferencing environments like Skype, Adobe Connect, or virtual worlds like *Second Life*, or Open Sim. In all of these spaces we see a combination of means of communication: video, audio and chat, video, audio chat and emoticons. In virtual worlds the human form is replaced by an avatar, which also changes the nature of the communication and, it has been argued, allows learners to become more confident in their use of language. It is argued that because the avatar is not the person himself or herself, but a computer generated representation (sometimes an animal or inanimate object), they are happier to be more experimental and prepared to make more mistakes.

A final part of this unit is to explore the use of embodied conversational agents (ECAs), best illustrated by the voice recognition tool Siri. This is an area of rapid development in the wider world with interfaces to technology increasingly becoming voice activated and response either output as text, in for example a voice-activated Google search, or the voice response of tools like Siri, or Cortana. We have also seen massive strides in the development of word processing software that will produce text from voice input. This has been accelerated by such tools arriving as apps on mobile phones and which work very much more effectively than they did in the recent past.

Virtual worlds lead us neatly into digital game playing which like many of the other areas discussed in this chapter has had its devotees and its detractors. In terms of the research base, one of the key devotees has been Thorne who argues, along with Cornillie and Desmet (2012) that there has been an increasing interest in the use of various types of digital games in language learning in recent years. This is evidenced in the literature and we have seen a number of recent overviews and introductions to the area, for example: Lai, Ni and Zhao, (2013) and Peterson (2010), as well as practical guidance from Stanley and Mawer (2011).

There has always been a tension between games that have been designed specifically for language learning, which although they are used regularly in class have not always captured the imagination of learners, and what are termed COTS (commercial off the shelf) games. In the course, as a practical activity we have explored virtual worlds, where we have played games together as well as looking at the video game Trace Effects (http://americanenglish.state.gov/trace-effects) that has been specially created for language learning. We also look at the role that serious games (Young et al., 2012) can play in supporting language development as a part of exploratory practice, or ESP. We finish off by taking our gaming out of the classroom into the wider world (Driver, n.d.; Holden & Sykes, 2013) and make use of the Internet and mobile technologies to solve a quiz and record the solving of it. The material is then brought back to the classroom and the students prepare for and do a class presentation showing their journey around Manchester. In doing this they bring together a range of skills that have been presented as a part of the course unit. In the most recent version of this unit, we have started visiting a local museum and exploring the ways in which language can be practised there. Materials are again brought back to the class for further work and discussion.

This brings the course unit to an end and the students write an assignment that brings together the three different elements of the course. They choose a specific context and suggest an issue that they want to address, they do a literature review to explore what others have said about the practice they are interested in and then they produce a lesson plan which brings the two earlier parts together.

Features and issues

The biggest issue facing any teacher who attempts to use technology in the classroom is the constant rate of change of technologies and the participants walking through the door. In a study that was conducted for Cambridge University

Press (2008a, 2008b) which explored the uses that teachers make of technology in their classrooms, we saw that classrooms where technology was being used were changing. Although we found that there was still a lot of evidence of what might now be termed multimedia labs which are specially booked for language classes, there was also an increasing use of technologies in the regular classroom. Quite often these classrooms were not well equipped and might have a single projector attached to a computer, or might be used by a teacher bringing in their own laptop, sometimes with a connection to the Internet, sometimes pre-preparing material and bringing it in on a portable device, like a USB drive. This work in classrooms is often linked to external tools where material is stored, or activities are carried out. These external tools might be an institutional VLE, or they might be a tool like a blog, or a wiki set up by the teacher for use with the learners where the teacher works to extend what they do in the classroom, or a 'flipped' activity so that the students prepare in advance for something that they will do in class. There is no doubt as I argue in my book (Motteram, 2013) that the landscape of activity has changed and as Warschauer and Healey (1998) argued a long time ago, many learners are no longer isolated in their local worlds, but have global access to a wide range of authentic language sources. Motteram et al. (2008a & 2008b) showed the broad opportunities that teachers have to blend and distribute learning, to be flexible, to access the real world and language in use. Learners need to develop their digital literacy; they need intercultural awareness, the development of autonomy and strategies to manage the wealth of available material.

Teachers are also changing. While on the MA at Manchester there is still a range of ages who do the course, they are increasingly mostly from the millennial generation. Each year I conduct an initial quiz with the students, asking about their own skills as teachers and what technologies they have available in their context. This is an interesting survey and I now present some highlights from the last two years of the onsite cohorts (2014 and 2015). The survey asks them about their 'Access to Technology', their 'Computer Confidence' and their 'Personal Computer Use'. I report on the responses of twenty-seven students in total. I also make some comments that I am aware of from the distance students who report access to technology in a different way.

These students come from a number of countries, or, if they are from the United Kingdom and have worked abroad for a time, work/ have worked in a number of different contexts. Typical countries where people work/ have worked include: China, various countries in the Middle East, various countries in south America, countries in Africa, Indonesia, Malaysia, Korea, Taiwan,

Pakistan among others. Twenty-one report having access to typical video play-back technologies like DVDs. Interactive whiteboards (IWBs) are less common with twelve students from the onsite cohort over the two years not having access to them. Informal discussion among the distance students revealed quite a high level of IWB use among that group, however. Access to smartphones seems to be growing among learner populations, although a lot of teachers point out that they are not allowed to use them with students in their classes. In 2015, ten teachers reported that their students had access, in 2014, only five teachers did. The use of online learning materials also seems to be growing, seventeen out of the eighteen teachers reported that their students had access to such materials, often through VLEs like Blackboard.

In terms of their own confidence in using computers, eighteen agreed that they were generally confident about using computers, eight were a little more cautious and one did not feel confident about computer use. Similar ratios felt confident to use word processors and to access the web, but there was less confidence expressed in using tools like spread sheets, databases and video conferencing.

In terms of personal use of computers, they all reported using the Internet as a source of information, twenty-three of them said that they accessed information on their mobile phones and used office based systems. Use of social media was less emphatic in its use with two people in 2014 saying that they did not use it and only sixteen people overall reporting that they used it frequently. The final question concerned digital games with only two people reporting that they spend some of their time playing digital games and nine people reporting that they do not play digital games at all. While a lot of these issues are predictable, it is useful to have a confirmation of the trends in the field and we do still see some of the students who have less access to technology in their teaching contexts and some who are still not confident in their personal use of technology.

Although the main teaching we do occurs in a traditional computer lab with twenty desktops arranged around the walls, a teacher's workstation connected to an IWB and a projector, in the last two years I have loaned students who did not have access to them, tablets, a mixture of Android and Apple devices. These were used on regular occasions during the course unit and comparisons were made to desktop and laptop devices. For each of the topics discussed, we explored how mobile devices could be used and looked at other issues that they raise in teaching languages. In order to gauge interest in the use of these tablets, I conducted a small survey at the end of 2015 to find out how they had been using the tablets and to see whether the students felt that we should put more emphasis on these mobile technologies in future versions of the course.

Ten out of a possible twenty-two students responded to the survey, and eight out of the ten were using iPads, two Samsung tablets. Some of the students in the class already had iPads, so this perhaps explains this discrepancy. The students reported using the tablets for activities one would typically expect on an academic course: taking notes, researching, tracking down and reading articles and communication. Five out of ten students carried the tablets with them every day and used them between two to four hours a day. In terms of whether use of tablets should predominate on the course, two students suggested that there should be a specific session on mobile technologies in the same way that other technologies are dealt with, others thought that the current balance was about right and only one thought that the tablets should be used throughout the course. It will be interesting to see how these views shift changes over time. The main technical issue with the tablets reported was that they tended to drop the Wi-Fi as the students travelled around the campus and I am not convinced that currently our Wi-Fi system would cope with twenty tablets accessing it at the same time, particularly if they are also using wireless on their phones and there are other people in the building also accessing the Wi-Fi. This will need some experimentation in future years.

Future directions

This current version of the course unit continues to grow and develop and will increasingly focus on developments in mobile technologies as these become more common around the world. It is also likely to try to broaden its reach to include more work on places where technology is not so readily available, but where mobiles make this possible. Other developments will include more emphasis on digital literacy and the revision of the unit on text reconstruction, which is an area that is not being pursued currently. This is likely to be replaced by developments in the role that artificial intelligence and big data are playing in digital technologies in general and more specifically in CALL.

References

Burbules, N. C. (1997). Rhetorics of the web: Hyperreading and critical literacy. In I. Snyder, (Ed.), *Page to screen: Taking literacy into the electronic era* (pp. 102–122). London: Allen and Unwin.

Cornillie, F., Thorne, S. L., & Desmet, P. (2012). ReCALL special issue: Digital games for language learning: Challenges and opportunities, *ReCALL, 24*(3), 243–256. http://dx.doi.org/10.1017/S0958344012000134

Develotte, C, Guichon, N., & Vincent, C. (2010). The use of the webcam for teaching a foreign language in a desktop videoconferencing environment, *ReCALL, 22*(3), 293–312. http:dx.doi.org/10.1017/S0958344010000170

Dudeney, G., & Hockly, N. (2012). ICT in ELT: How did we get here and where are we going? *English Language Teaching Journal (ELTJ), 66*(4), 533–542. http://dx.doi.org/doi:10.1093/elt/ccs050

Dodge, B. (1995). Webquests: A technique for internet based learning, *Distance Educator, 1*(2), 10–13.

Driver, P. (n.d.). Urban Chronicles blog: http://digitaldebris.info.

Garside, J. (2014). 300bn messages sent in UK forecast this year largely due to mobile flirting, *Guardian*, 5 August 2014. Retrieved from http://www.theguardian.com/business/2014/aug/05/1

Goldstein, B., & Driver, P. (2015) *Language learning with digital video.* Cambridge: Cambridge University Press.

Guichon, N., & Hauck, M. (2011). Editorial: Teacher education research in CALL and CMC: More in demand than ever, *ReCALL, 23*, 187–199. http://dx.doi.org/10.1017/S0958344011000139

Handley, Z. (2012). Investigating the use of interactive whiteboards during the pre-task phase of speaking tasks in the secondary English classroom. In L. Bradley & S. Thouësny (Eds.), *Proceedings of the EuroCALL Conference* (pp. 111–116), Gothenburg, Sweden. Research-Publishing.net.

Holden, C. L., & Sykes, J. M. (2013). Leveraging mobile games for place-based language learning. In P. Felicia (Ed.), *Developments in current game-based learning design and deployment* (pp. 27–45). Hershey, PA: Information Science Reference.

Hubbard, P., & Siskin, C. B. (2004). Another look at tutorial CALL, *ReCALL, 16*(02), 448–461. doi: 10.1017/S0958344004001326

Johns, T. (1986). Micro-concord: A language-learner's research tool, *System, 14*(2), 151–126. http://dx.doi.org/10.1016/0346-251X(86)90004-7

Kessler, G., Bikowski, D., & Boggs, J. (2012). Collaborative writing among second language learners in academic web-based projects, *Language Learning & Technology, 16*(1): 91–109. http://llt.msu.edu/issues/february2012/kesslerbikowskiboggs.pdf

Lai, C. Ni, R., & Zhao, Y. (2012). Digital games and language learning. In M. Thomas, H. Reinders, & M. Warschauer, (Eds.), *Contemporary computer-assisted language learning* (pp. 183–200). London: Bloomsbury.

Levy, M. (1997). *Computer-assisted language learning: Context and conceptualization.* Oxford: Oxford University Press.

Motteram, G. (Ed.). (2013). *Innovations in learning technologies for English language teaching.* London: The British Council.

Motteram, G., Slaouti, D., & Onat-Stelma, Z. (2008a) *Technology in ELT: The case study report*. Cambridge: Cambridge University Press.

Motteram, G., Slaouti, D., & Onat-Stelma, Z. (2008b) *Technology in ELT: Survey report*. Cambridge: Cambridge University Press.

O'Dowd, R. (2013). Telecollaboration and CALL. In M. Thomas, H. Reinders, & M. Warschauer, (Eds.), *Contemporary computer assisted language learning* (pp. 123–140). London: Bloomsbury.

Pennington, M. C. (1996). Writing the natural way: On computer. *Computer Assisted Language Learning, 9*(2–3), 125–142. http://dx.doi.org/10.1080/0958822960090205

Peterson, M. (2012). Learner interaction in a massively multiplayer online role playing game (MMORPG): A sociocultural discourse analysis, *ReCALL, 24*(3), 361–380. http://dx.doi.org/10.1017/S0958344012000195

Schmidt, R. W. (1990). The role of consciousness in second language learning, *Applied Linguistics, 11*(2), 129–158. http://dx.doi.org/10.1093/applin/11.2.129

Slaouti, D., Pennells, S., & Weatherhead, H. (2000). In search of a role for email and the World Wide Web in improving the writing of bilingual learners. In M. Beaumont & T. O'Brien (Eds.), *Collaborative research in second language education* (pp. 53–66). Stoke: Trentham Books.

Stanley, G., & Mawer, K. (2011). *Digital play: Computer games and language aims*. Peaslake: Delta Publishing.

Storch, N. (2005). Collaborative writing: Product, process, and students' reflections, *Journal of Second Language Writing, 14*(3), 153–173. http://dx.doi.org/10.1016/j.jslw.2005.05.002

Swain, M. (2000). The output hypothesis and beyond: Mediating acquisition through collaborative dialogue. In J. Lantolf (Ed.), *Sociocultural theory and second language learning* (pp. 97–114). Oxford: Oxford University Press.

Sweeney, P., & Moore, C. (2012). Mobile apps for learning vocabulary: Categories, evaluation and design criteria for teachers and developers. *International Journal of Computer-Assisted Language Learning and Teaching (IJCALLT), 2*(4), 1–16. http://dx.doi.org/10.4018/ijcallt.2012100101

Vanderplank, R. (2010). Déjà vu? A decade of research on language laboratories, television and video in language learning, *Language Teaching, 43*, 1–37. http://dx.doi.org/10.1017/S0261444809990267

Warschauer M., & Healey D. (1998). Computers and language learning: An overview, *Language Teaching, 31*(2), 57–71. http://dx.doi.org/10.1017/S0261444800012970

Wik, P., & Hjalmarsson, A. (2009). Embodied conversational agents in computer-assisted language learning, *Speech Communication, 51*(10), 1024–1037. http://dx.doi.org/10.1016/j.specom.2009.05.006

Willis, J. (1983). The role of the visual element in spoken discourse: Implications for the exploitation of video in the EFL classroom. In J. McGovern, (Ed.), *Video applications in ELT. ELT document 114* (pp. 43–55). Oxford: Pergamon/The British Council.

Woodward, T. (1986). Loop input-a process idea, *The Teacher Trainer, 1*, 6–7.

Woodward, T. (2003). Key concepts in ELT: Loop input, *ELTJ*, 57(3), 301–304.
Young, M. F., Slota, S., Cutter, A. B., Jalette, G., Mullin, G., Lai, B., Simeoni, Z., Tran, M., & Yukhymenko, M. (2012). Our princess is in another castle: A review of trends in serious gaming for education, *Review of Educational Research*, *82*, 61–89. http://dx.doi.org/doi:10.3102/0034654312436980

6

Balancing Theory and Practice

Developing Competent, Reflective CALL Practitioners

Eddy Moran
University of Stirling, Scotland

Introduction

This chapter introduces the module (course in other chapters of this book) 'TESP005 Introduction to CALL' that is offered as part of the Master of Science (MSc) TESOL (teaching English to speakers of other languages) in the Education Studies section of Stirling University's Faculty of Social Sciences. Computer-assisted language learning (CALL) has been an important element of our offering since 1993 when John Higgins, a founding father of CALL, joined what was then the School of Education's faculty. In describing this module, I hope to show the reader the underlying approach taken on the module to producing not only practitioners of CALL, but also competent, reflective language teachers.

Context

The Stirling MSc in TESOL

This module is offered as part of an MSc in TESOL that is largely aimed at training novice teachers who have little or no teaching experience. A high proportion of our students do, however, have experience and are attracted to take the course by the range of modules we offer. A distinguishing feature of the course is the large CALL component with a total of three different modules plus a Corpus Linguistics module (Corpora in Language Research and Teaching) on offer. Having three CALL modules allows a certain amount of specialization within CALL, so design and use of authored CALL materials is dealt with in the module 'Technologies in the 21st Century Classroom'. Use of a virtual learning environment (VLE) and online collaborative learning using Web 2.0 technologies such as wikis is covered in the module 'Designing and Implementing Online Language Learning'. This has also meant that decisions have had to be made on where to locate particular topics that could be placed in more than one module. For example, collaborative language learning could be included in the 'Introduction to CALL' module, but it is more logical to cover it in the 'Designing and Implementing Online Language Learning' module when we learn about groups working together in wikis.

As it was possible to do more than 50 per cent of the taught credits in CALL or Applied Linguistics, in 2012, we started offering named degrees – MSc TESOL (CALL) and MSc TESOL (Applied Linguistics) – in these areas so that our graduates could highlight the content of their degree. To be awarded the MSc TESOL (CALL), a student must have ninety taught credits (out of a total of 180) in CALL, which can also include corpus linguistics, and do a CALL-related dissertation. We have several students following this course at the moment, but the majority of students taking the 'Introduction to CALL' module are taking the main MSc TESOL with no particular speciality.

The MSc course has two core modules, 'Principles of Language Learning and Teaching' taken in the first semester and 'Research Methods in TESOL', taken in the second semester. The former module introduces the theoretical and research foundations of communicative language teaching (CLT) and a range of other key areas in second language acquisition (SLA) such as motivation, and learning styles and strategies. The latter module is a half module introducing research skills necessary for the completion of the dissertation. As the largest market for the MSc TESOL is novice teachers, we also have a 'Methodology' module, plus a 'Classroom Observation' module and a 'Microteaching' module. Other than this, options available include 'Grammar for TESOL', and 'Discourse Analysis'. Students who take the 'Introduction to CALL' module will, therefore, also be taking the core modules plus up to four other modules which are likely to include 'Methodology'. This means that there are frequent opportunities to integrate input from these modules into the CALL module or to introduce concepts which are then dealt with more thoroughly in second semester modules.

Who is the module aimed at?

The module is aimed at students who have two years teaching experience who want to gain a theoretical and practical understanding of the use of the Internet in teaching and learning languages. There are two reasons for the experience requirement. First, many of our MSc students have no teaching experience and they are directed towards pedagogical modules aimed at novice teachers. Second, personal experience shows that having some teaching experience is a definite aid in understanding and using online resources. The most experienced teachers appear to be those who are most creative with the resources and technologies we look at.

Aims and objectives of the module

The aim of this module is to provide participants with an understanding of the potential and limitations of computers and information technology in language teaching and learning, enabling participants to identify, select and critically evaluate educational software to enhance their teaching of English. The overarching intended outcome for this module is that, on completion of the module, our students will be familiar with the rationale for and actual use of the Internet for language teaching and learning in teacher-fronted, self-access and distance modes. Under this, there are two groups of intended outcomes. The first group relates to historical development, theory and evaluation. These outcomes require a critical awareness and understanding of CALL's historical development which in turn is closely entwined with the development of approaches to language teaching and learning (Bax, 2003; Warschauer, 1996). CALL practitioners also need an understanding of the relevance of theories of learning that underpin the design, use and evaluation of CALL materials. On a more practical level, teachers who use CALL must have an understanding of the potential and limitations of the use of communications and information technology in the language classroom and the roles of the teacher, the learner and the computer in the CALL class. This, in turn, requires the ability to identify, select and critically evaluate CALL resources. The second set of outcomes is related to pedagogy, online language assessment and distance teaching and learning. These involve familiarity with methods, resources and issues relevant to the teaching of reading, writing, listening and speaking. Students will gain knowledge and understanding of online language assessment. Finally, the module addresses key developmental and methodological issues in distance teaching and learning. To summarize, on completion of this module, our students should be able to apply online resources in a very practical way to second language learning and teaching while at the same time understanding what relevant theory and research suggests about how the appropriate use of these resources facilitates language acquisition.

Theoretical foundations

The approach to theory follows a view of CALL, propounded by authorities such as Chapelle (1997, 1998) or Doughty and Long (2003), in which it is clearly seen under a broader umbrella of SLA theory and research. There are three key areas that form the basis of the module's theoretical input. These are, first, the SLA theory covered in the MSc's core module on Principles of Language Learning and Teaching. CALL is firmly placed within a standard SLA paradigm covering the theory and research which forms the rationale for CLT: comprehensible input (Krashen, 1985), comprehensible output (Swain, 1995) and Long's (1985) interaction hypothesis. There is also a clear focus on behaviourism (Jordan, 2008; Skinner, 1974) as this was, historically, a driver of CALL materials development and use (Bax, 2003; Warschauer, 1996). It is also very necessary in understanding and evaluating even the most recently created online resources. The application of Web 2.0 technologies in online language learning has contributed to a growing invisibility of the software and a more 'real' learner-to-learner interactive language learning environment. It could be argued that this has increased the relevance of mainstream SLA theory and research to CALL. Second, we refer to the Constructivist (Jordan, 2008) and Social Constructionist theories (Vygotsky, 1978), which underpin the rationale for CALL software design. These are necessary to understanding the use and evaluation of software features such as help functions that scaffold learning or, for example, providing a theoretical rationale for learner control of software. Third, we spend some time on Dual Coding Theory (DCT) (Paivio, 1971) and research relevant to understanding use of multimedia CALL. While DCT is conceptually quite difficult to grasp, it is a basic requirement to understanding the strengths and limitations of multimedia features and the design of specific online resources. In addition to the above, theory and research covered in other modules is often referred to and this will be expanded on in the Features and Issues section below.

Course Description

Description of content week by week

The syllabus (see Table 6.1) gives a week by week account of the module content. This content conforms very closely to the intended module outcomes. The first five lectures cover the history of CALL and the learning theories associated with each stage of its development (Lecture 1), evaluation and use of web-based materials (Lectures 2 and 3), learner interaction and associated theory and research (Lecture 4) and use of online communication tools together with the associated theory and research (Lecture 5). Following this, content moves on to use of multimedia (Lecture 6), a focus on using online resources to teach the four skills (Lectures 7 and 8), online assessment (Lecture 9) and issues and techniques in distance learning (Lecture 10). Lecture 11 is used as a catch-up class and for review prior to the final assessment.

The first half of the module, while appearing to be strongly focused on theory and research, is actually very practical. This is because much of the theory and research has already been covered in their core module on SLA and they only need to be reminded of it and guided to apply it to an online learning context. Students link theory and research to actual resources and have to critically analyse both the theories and the materials. They examine online materials in detail and look for their limits. Experienced teachers enthusiastically dissect materials while less experienced teachers see these materials in a new light. The result can be a very satisfying experience in which participants develop a healthy cynicism about claims made by designers and publishers, but also begin to see potentials they were not aware of.

The second half of the module focuses on very practical design and pedagogical issues. Discussion of multimedia-related theory is probably the most difficult part of the module input. While the students will have covered the key SLA theory and research and may even have been quite aware of it before starting the MSc course, Paivio's (1971) Dual Coding Theory is completely new to them. This theory posits that the human brain has two different data processing channels for analogue and serial data and that to be effective, multimedia materials must have built-in redundancy in the way information is communicated.

On the other hand, the lectures on using online resources to teach reading, writing, listening and speaking are very practical and students can immediately see direct applications to their own teaching contexts. In recent years, technologies such as blogs have become an accepted part of many people's lives and have even become 'old hat', but most students have never created one and have not thought about using them in their classes. When they learn how easy it is to create a blog, or another online communication tool such as a discussion board, they are very enthusiastic to learn and to apply their ideas. For listening and speaking skills, module content focuses on Web 2.0 tools provided by the Center for Language Education and Research (http://clear.msu.edu/clear/) at Michigan State University. Their Rich Internet Applications such as mashups and audio drop boxes enable exciting opportunities for students to produce listening and speaking materials that can be used anywhere with a good Internet connection.

Online language assessment is a hot topic and more and more students have experienced this. Content here focuses on computer assisted language testing and computer adaptive language testing. It is also necessary to introduce concepts such as assessment validity and reliability, practicality, authenticity and test security. In the past two years, we have also looked at computer assessment of writing using the Educational Testing Service's Criterion (https://criterion.ets.org, 2015).

Finally, we look at teaching and learning language at a distance. This is also something which many of our students have experienced. Our Chinese students, in particular, may have done IELTS courses online. It is also something which the MSc students will have experienced as much of our delivery is blended. In this lecture, we look at the issues relevant to teaching and learning language at a distance and this necessarily includes discussion of how the technologies covered in the previous 9 lectures can be applied. We look at online learning communities, and how they can be developed and maintained. We also analyse our own blended delivery methods using examples of use of technologies from our own online MSc TESOL.

To conclude this section, the content of the module is a broad coverage of what teachers need to know to be competent in the use of online resources. At Master's level, it is necessary to have a strong theoretical component and this is certainly present. However, it is very practical and, depending on the context in which our graduates find themselves teaching, they come out of this module with the basic competencies needed to exploit the wealth of material available on the Internet.

Assessments

There are two assessments, a mid-semester essay (1,750 words) evaluating an online language teaching/learning resource, and an end of semester take away test. The mid-semester evaluation is an easy to understand task with a very clear link to the input on the first half of the module. It is quite possibly the first assessment that the students do on any of their modules, so it is important that it is grounded and practical. Many of our students will not have done anything like this for several years. The take away test consists of eight short answer questions (200 and 300 words) from which they choose six to answer. The questions address the complete range of input in the second half of the module and they have three days to do the test.

Table 6.1 Module content

Lecture	Topic	Content
1.	History of CALL	• Historical stages in the development of CALL • Theories underlying use of CALL at each of these stages
2.	Using the Internet for teaching and learning.	• Evaluation of web page design • Materials available on the WWW • Approaches to teaching and learning on the WWW
3.	Evaluation of online CALL materials	• Evaluation of language teaching websites
4.	Interaction in the CALL class	• How learners interact with CALL materials • How learners interact with each other in a CALL class • Differences between teacher-learner, learner-learner and learner-computer interactions • Advantages and limitations of using computers in language teaching/learning
5.	Computer-mediated communication	• Email • Chat • Discussion boards • Video conferencing • New developments in mobile learning
6.	Use of multimedia	• Underlying theory and research justifying use of multimedia • Specific design features related to use of multimedia
7.	Pedagogy 1: Reading and writing	• Designing CALL reading materials • Online versus hard copy reading • Designing CALL writing materials • Word processing versus pen and paper: changes in writing strategies resulting from use of word processing
8.	Pedagogy 2: Listening and speaking	• Designing CALL listening materials • Listening materials available on the WWW • Classroom/self-access uses of CALL listening materials • CALL and speaking: • Pronunciation practice. • Voice recognition. • Rich Internet Applications
9.	Online assessment	• Forms of online assessment: CAT and CALT • Examples of online assessment • Advantages/disadvantages of online assessment

(continued)

Table 6.1 (*cont.*)

Lecture	Topic	Content
10.	Issues and techniques in distance teaching	• Delivery modes • Methods • Tools • Problems
11.	Catch-up and summary of the module	• Review of theory and practice • Applications to independent and classroom learning

There are several reasons for using a short answer take-away test. First, it has excellent content validity as it directly tests understanding of what we cover in class. Second, we have a policy of diversifying assessment across the MSc. Third, it is very easy to mark and the students get their results back very quickly. It could be criticized on the grounds that it is a written test for a module that is fundamentally practical. However, student feedback has been very positive as they see it as a fair test that allows them to demonstrate their understanding of a range of issues while the short answer format forces them to focus on what is really important. They also view it as less work than an essay of similar word length; with the take away test, they are under pressure for 3 days, but with an essay they suffer anxiety for much longer.

Features and issues

Place in the overall curriculum and links to other modules

In this section, I shall discuss what are believed to be the strong points of the module, but also some of the difficulties we have encountered. The most obvious feature of the module is the state of the art nature of the content, but this is true of any CALL module. At Stirling, however, we have worked hard to place all our CALL modules within mainstream SLA theory and research and CLT methodological contexts so that students will see CALL as part of the big picture.

The module is standalone and does not require any previous knowledge of online learning and has no formal links to other modules. However, the whole MSc programme benefits if input in one module links to input on others so that students begin to take a holistic view of the MSc's content. Understanding of input on one module can be reinforced if it is applied in other contexts. For example, SLA theory and research can be applied in a methodology module.

There are several areas where input in this module links to other modules. These include:

1. Principles of Language Learning and Teaching
   a. The SLA theory and research mentioned above (comprehensible input, output and interaction)
   b. Corrective feedback
   c. Learning strategies
   d. Theories of motivation
2. Methodology
   a. Schema activation
   b. Receptive skills: top down, bottom up approaches, pre, while and post phases in lesson planning
   c. Productive skills: the writing process, information gaps in speaking activities

For each of these areas, issues arise in the evaluation and use of online resources. To illustrate how these links are exploited, we will outline a class activity in which Long's (1985) Interaction Hypothesis, particularly the concept of negotiation of meaning, is applied. This activity is done in Lecture 4, Interaction in the CALL Class. Students are put in groups of three or four and assigned to one computer for each group. One of the students is an observer who does not take part in the activity, but watches the others carefully and takes notes on the quality of language used and the roles taken by individuals. The students who are at the computer are given some storyboard and online quiz activities, that would be classified by Warschauer (1996) as Behaviourist CALL, to do as a group with a very brief introduction to how the activities work.

After a few minutes, the groups are brought together for a discussion of the interaction and discourse that has been observed. Almost inevitably, the observers report that what they hear at the beginning is quite rich in terms of the quality of the language, but this soon degenerates to single word turns, 'yes', 'no', 'right' and so on. The input in the core SLA module is then referred to and they are asked to apply this terminology to what they have observed. This hopefully results in them realizing that when the groups do not understand how to use the activities very well, when they are 'task inefficient', there is quite a lot of negotiation of meaning and, consequently, a richer quality of language. Subsequently, when the groups become 'task efficient', there is almost no negotiation of meaning and the quality of language is 'impoverished' as Windeatt (1986) termed it. None of this is helped by the roles group members usually take in which one person often dominates the keyboard. This leads into analysis of Behaviourist and Constructivist aspects of the material and the interaction that goes on with and around the material, actions a teacher can take to mitigate these problems and types of online resources that are more likely to facilitate interaction, communication and negotiation of meaning.

It has been found that there is a two-way relationship in this linking. The input on the SLA module makes it possible to apply theory and research in language acquisition in a CALL context. However, this application clarifies theoretical concepts for the students. For example, the concept of negotiating meaning might not be clear to an individual when first exposed to it in the SLA module. When doing this activity, though, they can actually see it in action.

A further example would be discussing the role of learner autonomy in software. This comes up in several lectures, but one simple example is asking students if they can give a theoretical rationale for learner control of a software feature such as the ability to control a video (e.g., pause or repeat using the video controls). With a little guidance, students usually come up with comments about cognitive learning strategies (Oxford, 1990) or theories of motivation such as Self Determination Theory (Deci & Ryan, 2002) or Attribution Theory (Weiner, 1986) which emphasize individual control of learning. Again, there is a recursive relationship with the other module because the students see the concepts in action.

Problems and solutions

The strong theory and research component has been a problem because it means there can be a lot of teacher talk. This problem has been addressed by practicing what we preach. Where possible, long periods of 'chalk and talk' have been replaced by video tutorials created with Camtasia (Techsmith, https://www.techsmith.com/camtasia.html). This has been popular with the students as the input takes much less time. Students consistently raise two issues related to their probable future teaching. These are the relevance of module content and the cost of accessing sites or buying licences. Module content is questioned because many of the sites we study are blocked in the students' home countries. This issue is dealt with by knowing and pointing out the alternatives offered by the government concerned. For example, YouTube (https://www.youtube.com/) is blocked in China, but they have a very similar alternative called Youku (http://www.youku.com/). The issue of cost has been dealt with by making it a guiding principle in content selection only to use free or very cheap resources. This also has the corresponding advantage of making the module a 'low overhead' course.

The technical skills required for this module are minimal and students have few problems related to the online environment. Students these days tend to be very comfortable working online and working with new software; they may not be technical wizards, but they are *digital natives* (Prensky, 2001). However, we occasionally get technophobic students who either get confused about how to use online resources or cannot see how the resources can be used. One may ask why they take the module, but often it is because for one reason or another, it is the only module available for them to take. The best solution appears to be in creating a spirit of peer support in the class where students are encouraged to help each other and not to be embarrassed about asking for support.

In an era of cost cutting and limited financial resources, technical support has suffered, but is still adequate. In the university, technical support for general hardware and software issues is centralized and if, for example, new software has to be installed, three weeks' notice has to be given and a form filled out to cover licensing and copyright issues. Support for learning technology is not quite so centralized and our learning technology unit has a learning technologist dedicated to education studies. This is one of the better aspects of support as the learning technologists are very committed to the use of technology in education and are very supportive of this particular module.

Finally, a key limitation of the software available is that we cannot use communications technologies such as Skype (https://www.skype.com/en/) in the computer rooms and we are not allowed to use webcams. We just have to work around this limitation. A further problem is headphones and mics. These are not supplied by the university as standard on each computer and students have to supply their own.

Future directions

The future development of this module is most likely to require changes in content and delivery driven by development of technology, market demands and financial constraints. Changes in content are likely to be related to the refinement and application of Web 2.0 technologies for language learning purposes. For example, the module does not currently address the potential uses of social media such as Facebook (https://www.facebook.com/) and this is a strong contender for future inclusion.

Delivery of module content is likely to become more blended. This is partly because online delivery using video tutorial is 'practicing what we preach', but also appears to have several advantages for the students and teachers. Students will get a more efficient, flexible and potentially more effective delivery of input, leaving them more time for practical skills development. In addition, packaging input in this way enables multiple use of materials by teachers. For example, input for the on-site MSc TESOL could also be used for the online version.

References

Bax, S. (2003). CALL – Past, present and future. *System, 31*(1), 13–28. doi:10.1016/S0346-251X(02)00071-4

Chapelle, C. (1997). CALL in the year 2000: Still in search of research paradigms? *Language Learning & Technology, 1*(1), 19–43. Retrieved from http://llt.msu.edu/vol1num1/chapelle/default.html

Chapelle, C. (1998). Multimedia CALL: Lessons to be learned from research on instructed SLA. *Language Learning & Technology, 2*(1), 22–34. Retrieved from http://llt.msu.edu/vol2num1/article1/index.html

Deci, E. L., & Ryan, R. M. (2002). *Handbook of self-determination research*. Rochester, NY: University of Rochester Press.

Doughty, C., & Long, M. (2003). Optimal psycholinguistic environments for distance foreign language learning. *Language Learning & Technology, 7*(3) 50–80. Retrieved from http://llt.msu.edu/vol7num3/doughty/default.html

ETS Criterion (2015). https://criterion.ets.org/criterion/Default.aspx?ReturnUrl=%2fcriterion accessed 25 July 2015.

Jordan, A. (2008). *Approaches to learning: A guide for teachers*. Maidenhead: McGraw-Hill International (UK).

Krashen, S. D. (1985). *The input hypothesis: Issues and implications*. New York: Longman.

Long, M. (1985). Input and second language acquisition theory. In S. Gass, & C. Madden (Eds.), *Input in second language acquisition* (pp. 377–393). Rowley, MA: Newbury House.

Oxford, R. (1990). *Language learning strategies: What every teacher should know*. NY: Newbury House.

Paivio, A. (1971). *Imagery and verbal processes*. New York: Holt, Rinehart, and Winston.

Prensky, M. (2001). Digital natives, digital immigrants. *On the Horizon, (9)*5. Retrieved from http://www.nnstoy.org/download/technology/Digital%20Natives%20-%20Digital%20Immigrants.pdf

Ryan, R. M., & Deci, E. L. (2002). An overview of self-determination theory. In E. L. Deci & R. M. Ryan (Eds.), *Handbook of self-determination research* (pp. 3–33). Rochester, NY: University of Rochester Press.

Skinner, B. F. (1974). *About behaviourism*. London: Cape

Swain, M. (1995). Three functions of output in second language learning. In G. Cook & B. Seidlhofer (Eds.), *Principle & practice in the study of language* (pp.125–144). Oxford: Oxford University Press.

Vygotsky, L. S. (1978). *Mind in society: The development of higher psychological processes.* Cambridge, MA: Harvard University Press.

Warschauer, M. (1996). Computer-assisted language learning: An introduction. In S. Fotos (Ed.), *Multimedia language teaching* (pp. 3–20). Tokyo: Logos International.

Weiner, B. (1986). *An attributional theory of motivation and emotion.* New York: Springer-Verlag.

Windeatt, S. (1986). Observing CALL in action. In G. Leech & C. Candlin (Eds.), *Computers in English language teaching and research* (pp. 79–97). London: Longman.

7

Training Teachers to Create and Use Materials for Computer-Assisted Language Learning

Scott Windeatt
Newcastle University, UK

Introduction

The way in which computer-assisted language learning (CALL) modules (*courses* in other chapters in this book) are updated by those who design and teach them will depend partly on changes in technology, partly on developing ideas about language learning and teaching, and partly on the perceived needs of the learners and their end-of-course reactions to what is taught. A Master's degree, however, is intended, and is likely, to have a long-term effect on the students. What is taught on a module, and how it is taught, will result in short-term learning effects, which can be identified and even measured during the course, but some of the knowledge and skills gained will almost certainly be revisited and developed once the course has finished. This is especially true of those CALL modules which are at least partly skill-based, and where ideas and confidence will develop through continued practice in using the technology. As a result, aspects of the course which may not have appeared to have much practical value when first encountered might nevertheless prove to be unexpectedly useful in the 'real world' (or the opposite, of course).

Learner reactions are routinely gathered at the end of a module or a degree course. Such immediate reactions, however, tell us little or nothing about the longer-term effects of a degree course, of an individual module, or of a particular aspect of a course, and evidence about those longer term effects is rarely available, either because little effort is made to gather it, or because of difficulties in maintaining or re-establishing contact with past students. This chapter describes a module on CALL which has developed over twenty-five years as part of a Master's degree. Differences between the first and recent versions of the module are considered, showing how the module has evolved in response not only to developments in technology and ideas about language learning and teaching, but also to changes in the background, needs and interests of students. Examples of immediate end-of-course reactions from the students are provided, as well as reactions from graduates who were contacted to explore the extent to which the longer-term aims of the CALL module appear to have been achieved. These reactions are then used to inform a discussion of the future direction in which technology-based modules on the degree might take.

Context

ALT8016 Computer-Assisted Language Learning is one of two technology based modules that are currently offered as options on the MA in Applied Linguistics and TESOL (Teaching English to Speakers of Other Languages) degree at Newcastle University. Both modules have developed over a period of twenty-five years, and, as CALL 1 and CALL 2, were originally offered as core modules on the MA in Media Technology for TESOL, and options on the parallel MA in Linguistics for TESOL. Other technology modules on the Media Technology MA included Video in Language Learning 1 and 2, and a module on Language Laboratories.

The MA degrees were originally aimed at practising language teachers and applicants were required to have at least two years' full-time teaching experience. There was also an attempt to maintain a balance between the proportion of L1 speakers of English and speakers of other languages in order to encourage the sharing of experience from as wide a variety of contexts as possible, and to provide the international students with as much opportunity as possible to interact with English-speaking students. This remained the case until a major reorganization took place within the university in the early 2000s, coinciding with a significant increase in the number of applications from the Far East – China in particular. These developments led eventually to the amalgamation of a number of degrees into a single MA in Applied Linguistics and TESOL, with separate pathways for experienced teachers and students with no teaching experience. The proportion of students from China in particular, in common with most, if not all, similar degrees in the United Kingdom has increased to the point where they now form the majority of students on the degree, as do students with little or no teaching experience. ALT8016, however, tends to attract mainly students with teaching experience.

Course description

The stated aims for the module are:

> Students will use a range of language learning software, and web-based resources for language learning. They will consider some of the advantages and limitations of using computers and the Internet for language learning, and will develop an understanding of how computer- and web-based resources can be used by language learners and teachers. Students will evaluate computer- and web-based language learning materials, and will learn how to design and produce their own web-pages and computer- and web-based language learning materials using basic authoring tools.

The intention is that students will bring to the module their experience of the language classroom as teachers and/or learners, together with ideas about language and language learning and teaching that they encounter in other modules in the degree, and will be encouraged to refer to that experience and those ideas when working with existing, and designing their own, computer-based materials. The expectation is that, in designing their own materials, they will have to examine in some depth their own ideas about teaching and learning, and in the process will develop their understanding both of what constitutes computer-based language learning material which is likely to be effective for a particular purpose and in a particular context, and of what the potential benefits and advantages are of using this medium. Above all, the aim is to help the students not only learn how to use particular computer-based resources and develop confidence in using the technology, but to acquire skills and knowledge that they will be able to transfer in new contexts once they have graduated, especially in response to developments in the technology that they will have to use.

The background knowledge and understanding the module aims to develop or build on includes:

- Experience of teaching and learning with CALL, and principally Internet-based, resources;
- An understanding of processes involved in learning and communicating in a second language;
- An understanding of some of the main current ideas about language teaching methodology;
- Familiarity with current CALL literature.

Those ideas are fostered though activities that include locating computer- and web-based resources that can be used for language learning and teaching, and evaluating their potential for teaching particular aspects of language by, for example, devising lessons or schemes of work for a defined group of learners in a particular context. This will involve decisions about whether the material is to be used in class or as part of a blended learning approach, consideration of what technology might be used, how the activities are to be managed and what preparation and support will be required.

The students' understanding of how ideas about language learning and teaching are embodied in computer-based language learning materials is further developed by practice in producing language-learning materials using software such as Hot Potatoes, Dreamweaver, Wordpress, Blogger or other web-design or blogging software. Multimedia materials are created using resources such as Movie Maker, Audacity, PowerPoint and Prezi, and a variety of other resources are used for particular purposes, introducing the students to as wide a range of resources as possible (Todaysmeet, Etherpad, Google Docs, etc.)

Assessment for the module requires the students to design, produce and pilot some computer-based materials and activities for language learning in order to demonstrate that they:

1. have developed sufficient skills to turn their ideas into practice by creating some computer-based language teaching materials and activities for delivery on the web and piloting them with users;
2. are able to (a) provide a clear description of the aims of their material; (b) with reference to relevant literature, explain the ideas about learning on which it is based; (c) discuss some of the possible advantages and disadvantages of using the computer and the Internet rather than another medium for this particular activity; and (d) discuss the results of piloting materials.

Features and issues

Evolution of the degree programmes

An important feature of this module is its focus on materials creation as a means of developing an understanding not only of how computer-based technology can be used for language learning, but also, more generally, of how ideas about TESOL and applied linguistics can be translated into practical resources for language learning and teaching. A particular motivation when the first version of this module was devised in 1990, however, was the limited range of commercial computer-based language learning materials, especially in languages other than English. Within the degree programme there was, at that time, a clear progression through the degree from this module, to a more advanced module in the second semester, when there was greater emphasis on evaluation of the student-created materials in use with learners, and then to the final piece of assessed work, which was a software portfolio – equivalent to a dissertation – in which the students were expected to bring together skills and knowledge gained in all of the technology modules, which consisted of two CALL and Video modules, and an optional language laboratory module. However, the use of technology was, above all, to be informed by the knowledge they had gained in the other applied linguistics and TESOL modules, as well as their experience as language teachers and learners. There was a clear focus on the practical application of ideas about language learning and teaching, and a logical relationship among and progression through the individual modules. This was the case until, as a result of wider changes within the university and despite the fact that numbers of applications remained healthy, the MA in Media Technology for TESOL, was subsumed into a larger MA in Applied Linguistics and TESOL degree in the early 2000s. This necessitated a reassessment of the technology based modules within the overall degree programme.

Early versions of the CALL module

Since the first version of the module the degree itself has undergone major changes. The number, nationality and background of the students on the degree have altered significantly, and, of course, the technology has developed, as has the nature and variety of available software and other language learning resources. The changing nature of the technology and associated software underlines the need for the module to focus on developing 'skills and knowledge that (the students) will be able to transfer to new resources', and those changes, as well as changes in the student intake, have therefore required an ongoing re-evaluation of the content of the module. In the first year it was offered (1990–1991), for example, the outline for the CALL 1 and CALL 2 modules (they were in essence envisaged as one large module taught over two semesters), was as follows:

Technical competence

Introduction to computers and the network: What is a computer? Switching on and off the machines. Logging in. Logging out

MS/DOS: Listing the contents of a directory. Changing drives. Formatting disks

IT literacy
  Word-processing: Starting the word-processor. Writing/deleting/inserting. Saving and loading text. Formatting text. Printing. Block copy/move/delete. Spellchecking
  Communications: e-mail and bulletin boards: Logging in. Reading messages. Sending messages
  Databases: Browsing. Searching. Printing
  Spreadsheets: Administration – budgets
  Concordancing: Searching. Printing. Types of corpora
Familiarization with existing language teaching software
  Introduction to CALL software: Software types. Running software.
  Authoring software
Evaluation of language teaching software and technology
  Software evaluation: Developing a software evaluation instrument
  Classroom observation: Techniques for classroom observation. Practice in using classroom observation techniques in CALL
Use of language teaching software with learners
  CALL in the classroom: Lesson-planning for CALL. Classroom
  Management and CALL
  Practising writing with the computer: Word-processing. Writing 'helpers'
  Practising speaking with the computer: Simulations
Design and creation of language teaching software
  CALL authoring software
  Programming in Microtext
  Desktop-publishing
  Graphics

Assessment for the two modules consisted of:

ASSIGNMENT 1
Development and application of criteria for evaluating CALL software

- Develop a set of criteria for evaluating software
- Explain your choice of criteria
- Evaluate your chosen criteria by using them to evaluate 2 pieces of software

ASSIGNMENT 2
  Write a program in Microtext
  or
  Prepare a collection of materials for one or more CALL programmes

ASSIGNMENT 3

Plan a lesson, prepare the materials, devise evaluation techniques, teach the lesson, evaluate it, and suggest modifications.

Developments in IT literacy

A major development over the years has been in the general level of computer literacy and the information technology (IT) literacy element in the early modules was first extracted and taught in a separate optional module (Communications and Information Technology), which was offered until 2002. It was also around that time that the Arts Faculty ended provision of an IT induction course for new undergraduates at the start of the academic year, in response to a rise in the basic level of IT literacy with which the new students, including those on our MA degree, arrived at the university. While the general level of IT literacy has continued to rise, however, there remain a number of gaps:

1. European Computer Driving Licence surveys completed by our MA students suggest a lack of confidence in dealing with security and privacy issues.
2. The same surveys show a lack of familiarity with spreadsheets, which is not as much of an issue as security concerns, but is nevertheless unexpected.
3. Experience of working with students in class suggests that an understanding of the relationship among drives, drive letters and folders cannot be assumed (especially among Mac users). This may not be an issue in everyday use, especially as the students' experience of computing is increasingly based on mobile technology, but it is important when creating materials, especially for the web, where an understanding of pathnames is required.

Recent versions of the CALL module

The original CALL modules are now taught as independent modules (i.e., there is no expectation that students on one module will necessarily do the other), and the current ALT8016 CALL 1 module (as discussed in the course description above) has the following aims:

Familiarization with existing language teaching software

1. Students will use a range of language learning software, and web-based resources for language learning.

Evaluation of language teaching software and technology

2. Students will evaluate computer- and web-based language learning materials
3. They will consider some of the advantages and limitations of using computers and the Internet for language learning.

Use of language learning software with learners

4. They will develop an understanding of how computer- and web-based resources can be used by language learners and teachers.

Design and creation of language teaching software

5. Students will learn how to design and produce their own web-pages and computer- and web-based language learning materials using basic authoring tools.

Assessment

The design, description, production and evaluation of computer-based language learning materials for delivery on the web.

The value of self-created materials

A major issue when courses were first provided for language teachers in the use of computers was the need – or otherwise – for a detailed understanding of the technology, and teachers often criticized the training they were given for concentrating on aspects of technology rather than pedagogy. While, as a result of the development of appropriate courses focusing on the pedagogical application of technology, this is no longer seen as an issue, a related question is whether there is a need for, and value in, training teachers to produce their own technology-based materials. On the one hand, apart from the self-contained computer-based courses that are available (such as Rosetta Stone and others specific to a particular country or first language), many mainstream language courses (e.g., Headway) now include supplementary computer-based materials for self-study use, or for use in the classroom on, for example, interactive whiteboards. In addition, the web is a rich source of material that teachers can use or adapt. Early training courses for teachers often included an introduction to programming languages such as BASIC, mainly with the aim of demystifying computer software, as it was not generally assumed that teachers would want to spend their time learning how to program in order to produce their language teaching software. Authoring software which allowed teachers to edit their own content into existing frameworks was seen as a potentially useful compromise in allowing teachers to focus on content, as they would if producing their own material on paper, without having to grapple with the intricacies of programming. Programs such as Storyboard, Gapmaster, Fun with Texts are early examples of such software, and Hot Potatoes is a more recent, web-based, example. Nevertheless, there has always been a demand among some of our MA students for the opportunity to create materials that move beyond the limitations imposed by such authoring programs, and there are potentially valuable insights to be gained from the process of translating theories and beliefs about language learning and teaching into practical materials. The problem, however, has always been to find software that can allow the exercise of such creativity, without requiring the students to become computer programmers (i.e., to allow them to create while focussing on the content rather than the technology). Over the years a wide variety of such software has been used.

Authoring software

One of the first such authoring programs we used was Microtext. This was text-based, ran under MS-DOS, was relatively straightforward to code, and capable of controlling a Laserdisc player. This was soon replaced by hypertext software – initially a Shareware program called Black Magic, which was cheap but unreliable, and then OWL (later Macromedia) Guide. Note that one consideration was whether or not software was affordable by the students. While it was provided free during the course, students naturally wanted to take copies of the software away with them. In this case the main choice was between Guide and Asymmetrix (now Sumtotal) Toolbook (which adopted a similar card-based approach to Hypercard on Mac computers). Both had similar functionality, but Guide was offered at a much more affordable price to educators. The attraction of both programs is that materials creation was basically menu-based, although there was a powerful scripting language (LogiiX in the case of Guide, Openscript for Toolbook) that could also be used. Development of Guide was halted in the late 1990s and it was replaced on our CALL module by Macromedia Authorware, which was icon- rather than menu-based, and if anything more complex than Guide, but supported by a strong community of users. In the meantime, the web became increasingly important as a means of delivering teaching material from the mid-1990s, and students were taught how to write web pages in Notepad and initially – bearing cost in mind – with free or cheap software such as HotDog or Netscape Navigator, but later with Dreamweaver, which was more expensive but still available, at that time, at a manageable educational price. Authorware had a web plugin, but was not designed for the production of web-based material, and when it was acquired by Adobe development was halted in 2007. Since then ALT8016 has focused on creating web-based materials, using Dreamweaver, Hot Potatoes, and a range of blogging and multimedia software.

The limited lifespan of computer-based materials

All language teaching materials become obsolete. Paper-based materials – textbooks – produced when the CALL modules were first taught in 1990 appear dated in content and approach now. Video materials produced by the students at that time look dated, as fashions and features of the environment have changed. Computer-based materials, however, probably age more rapidly than those in other media. Materials created in Microtext twenty-five years ago can only with great difficulty be persuaded to run on current Windows computers, and even then look hopelessly unattractive. Guide can be persuaded to run, but with some difficulty, as can Authorware programs, so while the content of some of the material created with these programs is still of value (some have been translated quite successfully into web pages) the original software is effectively no longer usable. The question therefore is whether, given that the actual material produced is likely to have a limited lifespan, the stated aim of helping 'the students not only learn how to use particular computer-based resources, but to develop skills and knowledge that they will be able to transfer to new resources, especially as the technology develops' has been worth pursuing.

Module evaluation

We routinely carry out end-of-course evaluation of our modules, and typical comments on the CALL module from students over the years have included:

> *Original version of the module: Selection of comments from 1990–1991 cohort*MS DOS etc.: Absolutely vital for the novice who has to be introduced to the hardware. It's also good for those who have 'half-knowledge' of computers as it fills certain preliminary gaps. Even those who are familiar with computer utilization, it's a good introduction to the network.
>
> Theory: The course suffers from a serious lack of theory … Students need to acquire the necessary skills but also need to be cautious and critical from the start.
>
> Practice: Would have liked to have done more on techniques for using software in the classroom.

Methodology: The general approach seems to work (talk then people working at their own rate) for most people.

Participants: There are problems with running a course for people with quite different levels of expertise (and interest?).

Theory: More articles and theories support!

Practice: More lessons on how to use computers for language teaching.

Recent versions of the module:

Selection of comments from 2012–2013 cohort

Materials production: Every session on ... Dreamweaver was of great use to me. / Practice with Dreamweaver was very useful.

Practice: The practical sessions given in applying what have been learned in the lessons have helped me to develop new knowledge in handling computers and give me innovative ideas on how to utilise computers for teaching and learning.

Participants: Different people have different level of computer skills, they may need different tasks.

Selection of comments from 2013–2014 cohort

Theory: It is a good balance of practical application and background reading and theory. I never felt confident that I could make my own website and this class not only taught me how to do it but helped me to apply that knowledge to real-world teaching.

Practice: This module gives us chance to practice teaching./ Practical contents are useful./ I like the fact that we get to practice everything we are introduced to./ I learnt a lot from this module that I can apply in my future career./ It also provides sufficient and useful feedback from peer and teacher right after the teaching practice.

Materials production: I enjoyed creating a website.

Long-term reactions to versions of the CALL module

On the whole, therefore, if the end-of-course comments are to be believed, the module has developed from the initial version into one that appears to provide what the students think they want and need. Given the aim of helping them develop transferable skills and knowledge, however, only information from post-course, and especially delayed post-course, evaluation, would help us confirm whether we had achieved that aim. Nevertheless we rarely attempt to carry out evaluation of that kind, mainly because, although we collect information about how to contact students once they have completed the degree, as most of them are young and mobile, both home and email addresses provided as contact details tend to change. The university's alumni database has not proved very helpful in maintaining up to date contact details. Social networks are less useful than might be expected, as many of our students are Chinese, they tend to use Facebook only while in the United Kingdom. Nevertheless during 2013–2014 we attempted to contact as many graduates as possible who had completed our MA degrees since the early 1990s.

Of the total number of students on the various Master's degree we have offered, by 2013 around 300 had opted for ALT8016 or earlier versions of this CALL module and we asked those we managed to contact, among other questions:

1. To what extent do you think the following aims of the module were achieved? Do you feel that, for yourself, some were achieved more successfully than others? Which?
   a) Students will use a range of language learning software, and web-based resources for language learning.
   b) They will consider some of the advantages and limitations of using computers and the Internet for language learning, and will develop an understanding of how computer- and web-based resources can be used by language learners and teachers.
   c) Students will evaluate computer- and web-based language learning materials, and will learn how to design and produce their own web-pages and computer- and web-based language learning materials using basic authoring tools.
2. Did your confidence in using technology improve as a result of doing the module?
3. How did you cope with creating your own computer-based materials?
4. Since completing the module, have you created, or do you think you will create, your own computer-based materials?

Replies from recent graduates included (names have been replaced by letters):

1. Were the aims achieved?
   M 2010–2011: *I think all three aims were achieved. I was able, for instance, to make my own Moodle-based materials for my software portfolio using Hot Potatoes.*
   S 2012–2013: *I certainly got an insight into different types of learning software and we considered advantages and disadvantages. The most important*

thing for me was to develop my own website – I am not really a technical person but I managed to put a website together without any problems. This has given me confidence to further develop this in the future – issue as always is time as it is not a priority in my context and therefore other things always seem to get in the way of developing more online materials. However, I think I have used Blackboard more than in the past as a result of the module.

L 2012–2013: *The module gave us an overview of what was available ... we did develop an understanding of how resources can be used ... The advantage and limitations were covered in the reading that accompanied the course and gave us an overview ... (Evaluating and designing material) was fully achieved, more than the other two aims ... This allowed us to research and develop our ideas beyond the course material.*

A 2013–2014: *Yes, I think the aims were achieved, though I'm not sure how to measure the extent. The second and third aims (advantages and limitations of the medium, evaluating and creating materials) stand out more in my mind.*

C 2013–2014: *I think I got a lot of new knowledge especially about new software that I can use to design my own webpage. However, it might take more time to learn about how to integrate more interesting materials to the webpage since I mostly just know about how to use Hot Potatoes software and Dreamweaver.*

2. Did their confidence improve?

S 2012–2013: *I am not usually good at technical stuff but once you got your head round Dreamweaver it was actually quite straightforward to use.*

L 2012–2013: *I think it has increased my confidence. Even though I was already using technology in my teaching it made me more adventurous to try other things. Learning more about the advantages and limitations on the CALL course gave me an understanding of when was a good time to use technology and for what tasks.*

A 2013–2014: *I feel I have a better understanding of how to evaluate materials and find quality resources online rather than just using technology for the sake of using it. My confidence using the computer in general is the same, but I have a lot more confidence in using Dreamweaver and Hot Potatoes software.*

S 2012–2013: *Yes, I am more confident.*

L 2012–2013: *I am more confident but I am also more critical of online learning resources and the exercises on CD-ROMs at the back of textbooks! I think if anything it has allowed me to understand what can be done with technology, the potential it has to be integrated into teaching but also the speed at which technology develops and changes.*

A 2013–2014: *Before the CALL class I would never have dreamed of trying to make my own website to use in my teaching. Now I feel I have a much better understanding of how to make one, as well as what kinds of materials to include on it. If I am ever in a more stable teaching situation where I teach the same types of classes year after year, I would now consider making a website to help distribute materials and information and have students be able to contact me.*

3. How did they cope with creating their own materials?

M 2010–2011: *I found Hot Potatoes limiting but far easier to use than Dreamweaver, which required more programming skills than I possess. It was extremely useful to see which resources are currently available and also how they could be applied to learning.*

S 2012–2013: *(creating materials was) when I learnt the most. I probably learn most from using Dreamweaver (rather than Hot Potatoes) and the video editing has been helpful.*

L 2012–2013: *I really enjoyed creating my own materials, however it was very frustrating at times ... However, it sparked my interest in web design and made me consider moving away from teaching and more into web design!*

A 2013–2014: *I liked having the chance to learn new software and really learn how difficult it can be to create materials. I have a greater appreciation for people who create online materials for language learning. It was helpful to be reminded not to focus too much on the technical difficulties, but to really be able to evaluate and defend the materials I was creating.*

C 2013–2014: *I think learning about how to use hot potatoes and creating my own webpage is something big for me. I wish I could learn about it more since I find it useful to make my teaching materials look exciting. However, since it was the first time I learned about creating my own webpage, thus, I found it was a bit frustrating when I had to design the background of the webpage. I felt that I spent most of my time for only designing the background and I didn't really pay attention to the materials. Then, I found that Dreamweaver is more interesting since you can integrate it with any software that you want to use.*

4. Are they likely to create their own computer-based materials?

S 2012–2013: *I'd like to have more time to do that but find it difficult to fit it all in. I have, however, used the activity created for the assignment with my current students (in slightly modified form). They seemed to cope alright with it, which was nice to see.*

L 2012–2103: *Yes, I would like to but I really think it depends on what lies ahead for me in terms of teaching. As a regular language teacher, it depends on what is predetermined by the school, in terms of material. I tried last year to develop Moodle sites with my own material and also proposed our own website/ blog for the school. However, I found that the number of students logging on to Moodle very low and the head of school didn't think any sort of site was necessary. I intend on trying again this year as I am teaching at another school which I hope is more flexible and open minded! I enjoy creating my own materials and I would only consider producing something digitally that can be used via a learning platform or interactively in class.*

A 2013–2014: *Possibly – I'm not sure I will go as far as making my own website but I suppose it depends on the type of classes I'm teaching and how much time I have for lesson preparation if I decide to put some of my class assignments online. At least now if I'm asked to create some online materials I will have much more of an idea of how to do it.*

C 2013–2014: *I might consider about it. Depends on where I teach.*

The reactions from recent graduates were therefore generally positive, including towards creating computer-based materials, though they were less certain about whether they would use those skills and knowledge to create such materials in future. The responses from students who had graduated in any year since the CALL module was first offered were then checked for evidence of whether and how they had been able to use what they learned on the module. No doubt as time passes it becomes more and more difficult to link current practice with specific past experience, so rather than simply looking at what effects students could link explicitly to the CALL module, the broader question was considered of whether their work after graduation involved using technology in a way that might have been influenced by the CALL module.

Reactions from past graduates

In addition to those above, the following is a summary of some of the comments from, or information about, around forty graduates from the circa 300 students who studied on versions of the CALL module between 1990 and 2014:

- 1992 Korea – past president of the Korean Association of Multimedia Assisted Language Learning
- 1992 United Kingdom – Course leader for BSc Computer Games Programming

- 1993 United Kingdom – Director of ELT Centre: *Immensely useful in the early stages of my post-MA career*
- 1993 United Kingdom – Writer of commercial CD-ROM based material for young learners in Malaysia
- 1995 Spain – English teacher in Spanish state sector: *Established interest in technology in language teaching, and especially applications of ICT; helped me develop interest in language teaching methodology in general. Stimulated my interest in digital technology in general*
- 1995 United Kingdom – Director of MA degree in TESOL with CALL
- 1996 Taiwan – Lecturer, University English Language Center: *The program was very flexible. Media technology is constantly changing and the program was not about specific programs or innovations, but about the greater concepts involved in teaching EFL … I remember Scott Windeatt emphasizing teacher education. I suggested that I was not interested in educating other teachers. I have since found that to be a vital part of my teaching life. Please stress this idea to young teachers and encourage them to share what they learn with others.*
- 1997 Brazil – Course coordinator and English teacher at Cultura Inglesa: using CALL and writing materials (e.g., online concordancer)
- 1998 United Kingdom – Part-time learning technologist
- 2000 Taiwan – English teacher in a public high school: using multimedia materials
- 2000 Thailand – University lecturer teaching CALL courses
- 2002 United Kingdom – Training university staff in the use of technology: *I was also able to get into online materials creation … and e-tutoring … I now work in a UK-facing unit and deliver staff training on the use of technology in teaching, manage projects which research aspects of technology in teaching/academia, organize events which bring together e-learning practitioners, and consult on the development of an in-house authoring tool – and I still do a bit of materials-creation. I liked designing online materials in Dreamweaver and Authorware. I liked the creativity of all the tech modules of the course. (The course) gave a good preparation for online materials creation – the thinking process you go through – e.g., why use technology for this learning outcome? What do I want to achieve? How best can I achieve it? How can I measure outcomes? The dissertation (creating some online materials, explaining and justifying the rationale behind them, testing and evaluating them) was the most important part of the degree for me as it has had the most impact on my work and thinking. The basic lessons learnt in those technical modules about*

good practice, instructional design, pedagogy in relation to technology were good lessons – and they stand the test of time even now, when technology has moved on so much … How to use the internet effectively for language teaching and understanding how to use the internet for research. These were basic lessons in digital literacy and still have relevance.

- 2004 Taiwan – Running my own private English school: *(the course) inspired me to infuse authentic media in the ESL classroom. YouTube is very handy!!*
- 2006 Japan – Teacher. *Using Hot Potatoes to teach vocabulary*
- 2007 Canada – *Developing commercial materials for online language learning*
- 2010 China – Managing a private language school: *My employer is currently developing new materials for the iPad, and I'm attempting to influence this development process based on work I did in CALL modules.*

A number of others have since been in touch, most of whom are teaching on in- or pre-sessional courses in the United Kingdom and routinely use computer- and web-based materials.

Of the other circa 250 students a number have completed or are completing PhDs, nineteen in the area of CALL. Of the others:

- Experience (and information from their peers) suggests that many (most) are language teachers (who may or may not be using CALL).
- Two are translators in Spain.
- Another runs a chain of language schools in Brazil and Ecuador.
- One runs a bed and breakfast in the Lake District.
- One is a life coach.
- Several have retired.

Conclusions

What, then, does our post-course evaluation tell us about both the short- and longer-term effects of the CALL module?

- We only have evidence from a relatively small proportion of graduates – perhaps 20 per cent.
- Most of those we were able to contact are making use of CALL.
- Some were able to link their use of CALL directly to what they had learned on the CALL module.
- For most of those we were able to contact the benefits of the degree have been significant.

- For some the degree and the CALL module have shaped their future career.
- For the others, however – the majority, whom we were unable to contact – the long-term effects of the degree or of the CALL module remain unknown.

Any conclusions can only be tentative in the absence of information from so many past students, but the fact that feedback is available from past students stretching back over so many years is useful, and on the whole supports the view that the module is likely to have at least gone some way towards achieving its aims, at least insofar as most respondents appear to have made some use of what they learned on the module, and have continued to develop an interest in the use of technology for language teaching.

Future directions

The aim of this chapter was to describe the current CALL module, discuss how it had changed since its inception, consider evidence as to its effectiveness in achieving its aims and its long-term effect on participants and identify how it might develop in future. While the technology itself has changed significantly over the years, the basic aims of familiarising students with the technology, developing their confidence in using it with language learners, exploring the possibilities and potential drawbacks of the medium through evaluating and using current software and through developing their own materials and so developing knowledge and skills that they can transfer as the technology develops still seem relevant. There is evidence from the immediate post-course evaluation we carry out that the majority of the students who chose this module feel that some or all of these aims have been achieved. Evidence from long-term post-course evaluation is more equivocal, mainly because of the difficulty in maintaining or re-establishing contact with past students. Nevertheless most of those students who were contacted have made use of computer-based materials in their work, some specifically identified the influence of what they had learned on the module, and, although most had not created their own materials using anything more complex than software like Hot Potatoes, a few had gone on to produce software of their own, or to teach others how to produce software. To what extent the module directly influenced their subsequent use of technology is hard to establish (they might have gone on to work with computers whether they had done the module or not), but there is evidence that the module had some positive longer-term effects, and that for those students we were able to contact, the module had met a need and an interest which they continued to develop.

In terms of the specific focus on creating materials, the emphasis within the technology modules on the degree has changed. Until relatively recently students who studied the first CALL module (ALT8016) would then automatically move on to a second CALL module which would also involve creating materials, but with a greater emphasis on evaluating the materials as they were used by learners. However, the second module is now independent of the first, has been renamed 'e-learning for languages' and deals with a wider range of topics such as virtual learning environments, the management of online courses, mobile-assisted language learning, computer-based language testing, automatic feedback on spoken and written English and teacher training. This is partly due to the fact that, while there is still interest among the students in creating their own computer-based materials, the range of computer-based resources available for language learning and teaching is far broader than when the CALL modules were first conceived, and commercially produced software now sets a standard of professionalism that MA students are generally unable to match. ALT8016 will therefore continue to focus on materials production. However, while Dreamweaver will continue to be offered as an option in the immediate future, more straightforward ways of creating web-based materials will also be offered, allowing consideration of the benefits and drawbacks of greater power and flexibility as opposed to ease of use of these different resources. In addition, the module will increasingly need to emphasize the implications for the design of materials intended for use on mobile technologies rather than desktop or even laptop computers.

However, although technology is clearly central to these modules, the main concern is its application in language learning and teaching. Developments in technology and in ideas about learning and teaching are what govern changes in the CALL modules. The modules also tend to change as the module leader's ideas about teacher training change. The approach in the modules has always been based on principles of social constructivism in that the students learn by doing, by working with each other and by learning from each other – and the teacher, in turn, learns from the students. A number of variations on this approach have been tried over the years, including a loop-input approach (Woodward, 1991), problem-based learning (Hmelo-Silver, 2004) and critical thinking skills (Krathwohl, 2002). Given the growing interest in and importance of online learning and MOOCs, the next approach to investigate in some detail will be that of Communities of Inquiry (Garrison, Anderson, & Archer,

2000), where fostering different kinds of presence among students when they interact during the course may encourage more active participation, and provide evidence of the extent to which their thinking develops as a result of that interaction. Modules such as these therefore provide an opportunity, not just for the students, but for the module leader to develop ideas about learning and teaching.

References

Audacity 2.1.0. (2015). [Computer program]. Retrieved from http://audacityteam.org/

Black Magic 1.20. (1990). [Computer program]. Ntergaid.

Choy, S., & Cheah, P. (2009). Teacher perceptions of critical thinking among students and its influence on higher education. *International Journal of Teaching and Learning in Higher Education*, *20*(2), 198–206.

ECDL Foundation. (n.d.). *Digital literacy survey*. Retrieved from http://www.digitalliteracy.eu/

Etherpad [Computer program]. Retrieved from http://etherpad.org/

Garrison, R., Anderson, T., & Archer, W. (2000). Critical inquiry in a text-based environment: Computer conferencing in higher education. *Internet and Higher Education*, *22*(2–3), 87–105.

Blogger [Computer program]. Retrieved from https://www.blogger.com/

Google Docs [Computer program]. Retrieved from https://www.google.com/docs/

Guide 3.1 [Computer program]. OWL International Inc.

Hmelo-Silver, C. E. (2004). Problem-based learning: What and how do students learn? *Educational Psychology Review*, *16*(3), 235–266.

Hot Potatoes 6.3.0.5 [Computer program]. Retrieved from https://hotpot.uvic.ca/

Krathwohl, D. R. (2002). A revision of Bloom's taxonomy: An overview. *Theory into Practice*, *41*(4), 212–218.

Microsoft. (2012). Movie Maker 12 [Computer program]. Retrieved from http://windows.microsoft.com/en-gb/windows-live/movie-maker

Microsoft. (2013). PowerPoint [Computer program]. Retrieved from https://products.office.com/en-gb/powerpoint

Microtext [Computer program]. National Physical Laboratory.

Prezi [Computer program]. Retrieved from https://prezi.com/

Todaysmeet. (2015). [Computer program]. Retrieved from https://todaysmeet.com/

Toolbook 11.5 [Computer program]. Sumtotal. Retrieved from http://tb.sumtotalsystems.com/index.html

Woodward, T. (1991). *Models and metaphors in language teacher training*. Cambridge: Cambridge University Press.

Wordpress 4.2.2. (2015). [Computer program]. Retrieved from https://wordpress.org/

8

Preparing CALL Professionals

A Survey Course in a CALL Degree Programme

Greg Kessler
Ohio University, USA

Introduction

This chapter describes an introduction to computer-assisted language learning (CALL) course at Ohio University that is required as part of the linguistics department Master's degree programme in applied linguistics. The course relies upon a foundational understanding of linguistic and second language acquisition (SLA) principles and incorporates aspects of research, theory and hands on practice in an integrated manner during each class meeting. While this class is a requirement for all MA students in the department of linguistics, it also attracts students from a variety of other disciplines, including teacher education, instructional technology and modern languages. The course is a single component of a series of five CALL courses, CALL certificate programme, workshops, conferences and activities related to CALL at Ohio University.

Context

Computers in Language Teaching I (Linguistics 5510) is one of twelve required courses that comprise the two-year Master's degree programme in applied linguistics at Ohio University. This series of courses is designed to provide a balance between theory and practice and range from foundational linguistic courses such as syntax, phonology, morphology and pragmatics to courses focused upon language teaching, including pedagogical grammar, pedagogical phonology, teaching reading and writing and teaching methods. This course is the first in a series of five CALL courses. The other four courses include: (1) a CALL practicum course that offers students an opportunity to get hands on experience teaching extensively within CALL contexts, create materials for a real world context or participate in a CALL related research project; (2) CALL Research Methods; (3) Audio and video for language learning; and (4) Interactive multimedia materials design for language learning. Computers in Language Teaching I is designed in a manner that reflects this programmatic balance and relies upon students' familiarity with foundational concepts in linguistics. As a result, there is much less attention to individual technologies and more focus upon conceptual awareness of how the use of technology influences language learning as well as language use throughout society. I have elaborated on the importance of such understanding in many previous publications (Kessler, 2012, 2013, 2015).

The students who take this class have generally spent little time thinking critically about the influence that technological innovations have had upon communication and society (Kessler, 2010). They have little academic experience reflecting critically upon the role that technology should play in the classroom. In fact, most of them have had limited experience using technology as a significant portion of their own learning in general. They have had even less experience using technology for language learning. However, like most people today, they are all comfortable, confident users of a variety of technological solutions for their own personal and social needs. Consequently, it has been beneficial to frame the course in a manner that presents these technologies as one component of an emerging pedagogy that relies upon the ubiquitous use of technology as a social tool to inform language teaching and learning practices. As a result there is a good deal of attention focused upon how the ICT social tools that we take for granted within our networked social lives can be leveraged in the language classroom. Each week alternates between a reading and a video lecture or other featured talk. These tend to be freely available archived recordings of recent CALL related keynote or plenary talks delivered by experts in the field. By incorporating such talks into the curriculum, students are able to gain insight into the most current and thought provoking topics being discussed in the field. (See Appendix A for the course syllabus including the list of readings and talks.) During Spring semester of each academic year, we also host a CALL conference that brings many of these same highly valued speakers to our campus so that the students can further benefit. The following includes some more details about the nature of the course.

Course description

Introduction to computers for language teaching is a survey course that serves as an introduction to the field of CALL as well as the extensive series of other CALL courses offered at Ohio University that lead to the certificate in CALL. The course is required for all Master's degree students in the linguistics department at Ohio University although it is also attended by students from other departments as well. The course presents students with a breadth of topics related to technology and language, including the influence of technology on communication and social behaviour, the use of technology for managing and delivering instruction, the use of technology for connecting language learners with speakers of the target language and the use of technology for exploring the target culture. Of course, many of these topics are changing constantly, thus the course is designed to respond to acknowledge and reflect upon such changes. This flexibility is also present in the theoretical disposition of the course. The material draws from the breadth of disciplines some have presented as the diverse lineage of CALL (Levy & Stockwell, 2006).

In spite of these changes, there are some fundamental topics that remain constant from year to year in this course. Many of these have been retained since they were incorporated in the class during the use of the textbook, *New Perspectives in CALL for Second language Classrooms* (Fotos & Browne, 2004). Such topics include identifying, evaluating and creating instructional media, materials, tasks and environments as well as a variety of decision-making processes related to the design of instruction. Such decisions may involve the sequencing of activities, seating arrangement of students, procedures for designing groups as well as choosing which tasks are best aligned with a particular form of technology. This is, of course, just a sample of many similar decisions that instructors need to make on a regular basis, particularly as they are designing new courses. Such decisions are also the foundation of an instructors' practice and it is important that future teachers are given opportunities to consider them as well as the potential outcomes.

Features and issues

Focus on role of technology

The course is constructed with a conscious focus on the role of the computer within instruction. Throughout the course there is a reminder that the computer functions at the centre of the learning experience that also involves students, instructors, materials and pedagogical considerations as recommended by Levy and Hubbard (2005). This focus does not result in a technology-centric course, but provides a critical lens through which the course is filtered. Such an awareness is important for future teachers as well as future CALL experts and specialists as described by Hubbard (2008). Students in this class are guided towards considering future careers in these roles throughout the CALL experience at Ohio University.

Balance of theory and practice

Students learn about the history of CALL research, theory and practice in this class. They are provided with numerous opportunities to explore a variety of perspectives on CALL and reflect on how these ideas may influence contemporary practice. This is a difficult balance to achieve, but this course is very intentionally designed to maintain a balance between theory and practice such that we read theoretical, research-based and conceptual papers in preparation for classes in which we explore the ideas in these articles through hands-on practice. This arrangement allows these theoretical and research based concepts to be more salient than they would be otherwise. Further, by combining these activities there is less monotony than one might encounter in a theory only class.

Each week there is equal time devoted to gaining hands-on experience creating CALL materials, tasks and activities and discussing CALL theory and research. The theory and research topics are used as a springboard for the more practical aspects of the class so that students may explore a topic such as learner autonomy by reading a research paper on that topic and then engage in a discussion about that article. Following this discussion, students will create an activity that is intended to promote the principles of autonomy. This activity will incorporate a tool or resource that is part of the focus of that day. Many of the topics, materials and practices gleaned from these daily activities are ultimately included in students' curricular development projects that serve as the penultimate and cumulative project for the course.

Curricular development project

All the activities in the class are designed to inform the group based curricular development project. This project is cumulative in that students generally incorporate each of the previous activities they have created throughout the course. Students who choose to create wholly new materials generally want to gain more experience in the area of materials development. These projects are designed around authentic teaching contexts that need to be defined in detail by the students in each group. In some cases the students have background knowledge of and/or experience teaching in the particular context. In many cases these curricula will be used in the near future within these contexts. These projects are designed around the eight conditions for optimal language learning environments identified by Egbert, Hanson-Smith and Chao (2007). These eight conditions include:

1. Learners have opportunities to interact and negotiate meaning.
2. Learners interact in the target language with an authentic audience.
3. Learners are involved in authentic tasks.
4. Learners are exposed to and encouraged to produce varied and creative language.
5. Learners have enough time and feedback.
6. Learners are guided to attend mindfully to the learning process.
7. Learners work in an atmosphere with an ideal stress/anxiety level.
8. Learner autonomy is supported. (p. 5)

These projects provide an overview of the course as well as a significant portion of the actual materials that would be used in the proposed course. In addition to the eight principles, the projects must involve aspects of learner training, which has been identified by some researchers as a critical often overlooked area (Hubbard, 2004; Kolaitis, et al., 2006). The students present the curriculum project at the final class meeting. The projects are evaluated according to an evaluation rubric designed around these eight conditions. This rubric is included as Appendix B. Readers may be interested in a study that elaborates on the design and implementation of this curricular design project and the use of this rubric to evaluate the effectiveness of meeting these eight principles (Kessler & Bikowski, 2011).

Open source focus

This course relies heavily upon media, instructional materials, resources and software that is freely distributed and open source under the GNU Project public licensing, creative commons or distributed through organizations such as the Center for Open Educational Resources for Language Learning (COERLL) at coerll.org.

This is an intentional decision not only as a best practice for the course itself, but also to expose future teachers to these practices. With the limited funding available for technology in education, it is becoming increasingly important to identify cost saving approaches. It is also important to help these future teachers understand the value that they bring to the world of technology as informed and involved users and potential contributors in this shared responsibility culture.

Evolving tools, practices and expectations

One topic that is frequently addressed in this course is the potential of other freely available tools, such as those offered by Google, and are commonly referred to as perpetual beta. These tools are not released with version numbers such as more traditional commercial software (e.g., Windows 8, or Netscape 3.0). Perpetual beta software can change dramatically with no indication to users. As a result, it is important to help those who are less likely to experiment with this kind of software on their own. This course is designed to embrace the perpetual beta paradigm. As new tools emerge, the course can diverge from anticipated activities to explore the potential of these new contexts.

Constructivism

The course is built upon SLA and constructivist principles. Many of the tools and activities that are explored have been selected based upon their potential to support collaborative and constructivist practices. Such tools and practices are familiar in our personal and social lives and offer great potential for meaningful, engaging and authentic language practice (Kessler, 2013). It is important that constructivism is not only discussed, but also actually practised in the class in order to give future teachers opportunities to reflect upon such practices. One example of the focus on these practices is the collaboratively designed and implemented constructivist midterm exam. This exam functions as a review of the content addressed during the first half of the course. The second half of the course is largely focused upon the curricular development project. The midterm involves each student creating a collection of ten questions, including five that they are confident and comfortable answering and five about which they are less confident. Questions should vary between big picture theoretical/conceptual topics to specific discreet topics. Students are then placed in groups of four or five members to compile these questions and answer them within the group. These are posted on a collaboratively shared site so that all students can see the questions and answers. The instructor selects twenty-five questions from this collection that will be included on the test. If any important topics are not included, the instructor will add them to the collection, but this rarely happens. Since the class is capped at twenty-five, this is typically the full size of the class. Students have all the original questions to study. On the day of the exam, students enter the class and choose a number from one to twenty-five. This is the question a student will answer. They have the opportunity to trade once if this one question is problematic for them. During the exam everyone is asked to elaborate on topics so that we can develop a deeper understanding. Consequently, students leave this exam knowing more than they knew when they entered. Many former students have told me that they have continued this practice in their own teaching.

Many other collaborative tasks are practised on a regular basis in this class. These serve as a model and an opportunity for these future teachers to experience collaborative learning, a practice that they have often heard about but had little to no experience with as a student (Kessler, 2010). These collaborative language learning practices and materials can be used to support and promote autonomous abilities for individuals to be productive and successful members of group project based learning. In order to promote such practices, the future teachers in this class participate in a group curricular design project. This project is specifically situated in an authentic teaching context that is explicitly described by the group. The importance of understanding how to address the realities of these specific contexts is important in considering the design of instructional materials, practices and tasks. Further, this practice promotes an understanding of situated learning.

Building confidence and troubleshooting

I believe that it is important for instructors to develop the ability to identify challenges associated with their pedagogical approach or practice as well as a particular technology that may function within that practice. Consequently, it is important to prepare these future teachers to do some basic troubleshooting. This class begins with an introduction to the functioning of the Apple operating system, including creating, saving and finding files and opening, closing and sizing windows. This is essential to prepare students who are unfamiliar with the Apple computers that we have in our classroom computer labs. It also serves as a reminder of how we may need to introduce some basic functions to students when working in unfamiliar new contexts. On this first day we also learn about the hardware components of a computer. The instructor dismantles a desktop computer and identifies each part, including a description of the function of the part as well as the potential for needing to upgrade or replace it. A small group of students then reconstructs the computer while identifying each piece. These students are generally recruited based on a lack of previous experience with such activities. This activity helps to demystify the computer for these future teachers. It also opens the door for the kinds of troubleshooting they may need to do in the future when they are expected to operate on a limited budget.

A portion of each class is devoted to troubleshooting technology and pedagogical situations on an as-needed basis. There is no expectation for students to become technological experts as a result of this experience, but they are able to develop a higher comfort level with addressing technological challenges. Such challenges may be encountered in a variety of educational situations, including classroom instruction, preparation, feedback or other correspondence with students. In most cases these issues are rather simple commonplace issues that any confident modern computer user can address without concern such as installing plug-ins, adjusting application preferences or effectively connecting peripheral devices. Sometimes these can be a bit more challenging, including hardware issues such as adding RAM or replacing a computer battery.

Future directions

This course has certainly evolved in significant ways over the years. When I began teaching the course in 2004, the essential requirement was that students should be able to demonstrate some reasonable mastery of the various software applications included in Microsoft Office. Students were tested upon their ability to adhere to established expectations of word processing conventions. They were also expected to be able to enter data into spread sheets and manipulate formulae in ways that illustrated their mastery of Microsoft excel. PowerPoint was touched on in a peripheral manner insomuch that students had to use it to give a final presentation. The other aspects of the Microsoft Office suite (that could arguably offer a variety of language teaching opportunities if repurposed) were largely ignored. Today the ability to repurpose these tools is the only remnant of that original class. Students are generally surprised to learn that they can embed audio and video within Microsoft Word to create more media rich content. However, it is the repurposing of the social tools (e.g., Facebook, Twitter and other emerging socially constructed contexts) that surround us that is most exciting looking forward.

These social tools have become so ubiquitous in our lives in recent years that it is difficult to imagine how different the world was prior to their arrival. We can crowdsource feedback. We can join communities of specific interest in any number of target languages. Within these communities we can share our thoughts on any number of topics as we develop language abilities in authentic and meaningful social contexts. We not only have the ability to interact with numerous target language speakers and cultural informants around topics of common interest across the globe, but we can also expect that they have reciprocal interest in participating. These tools have reshaped government, business and many other domains across society. Clearly, these are the tools that our future teachers should be prepared to integrate into their instruction. However, the tools that we are familiar with today are unlikely to remain as they are for long. We are still in the nascent days of social media and we should anticipate dramatic changes moving forward. As these social tools evolve it will be fascinating to experiment with their use across a variety of language teaching, learning and practice contexts. We can anticipate that we will continue to develop new pedagogical practices as we experiment with these new technologies.

It is easy to imagine future tools that have not yet been imagined today taking prominence. I feel that it is important to prepare future teachers to critically evaluate these potential tools and reflect upon their potential within the constructs of language and culture teaching, learning and practice. In order to do so, we explore emerging tools on a regular basis. Typically these tools present new ways to interact with, visualize, gather or share information. While they do not tend to focus upon language learning, they are generally social and intended to support a variety of forms of communication. This course helps students to recognize the potential for these social and communication tools in language teaching, learning and practice contexts. Students are not only encouraged to consider the use of these tools in language teaching, but they are also required to integrate these practices into their curricular projects. This requirement guides them towards experimenting with these new and emerging contexts in ways that can inform their future use. As these social practices evolve, new teachers who are willing to experiment will likely identify new practices that can leverage these tools most effectively.

References

Egbert, J., Hanson- Smith, E., & Chao, C. C. (2007). Introduction: Foundations for teaching and learning. In J. Egbert & E. Hanson-Smith (Eds.), *CALL environments: Research, practice, and critical issues.* (2nd ed.) (pp. 1–18). Alexandria, VA: TESOL.

Fotos S., & Browne, C. (2004). *New perspectives in CALL for second language classrooms.* Mahwah, NJ: Lawrence Erlbaum Associates.

Hubbard, P. (2004). Learner training for effective use of CALL. In S. Fotos & C. Browne (Eds.), *New perspectives on CALL for second language classrooms* (pp. 3–14). Mahwah, NJ: Lawrence Erlbaum Associates.

Hubbard, P. (2008). CALL and the future of language teacher education. *CALICO Journal, 25*, 175–188.

Kessler, G. (2010). When they talk about CALL: Discourse in a required CALL class. *CALICO Journal, 27*(2), 376–392.

Kessler, G. (2012). Preparing today's teachers to use tomorrow's technology tools. In G. Kessler, A. Oskoz, & I. Elola (Eds.), *Technology across writing contexts* (pp. 213–236). CALICO Monograph.

Kessler, G. (2013). Collaborative language learning in co-constructed participatory culture. *CALICO Journal, 30*(3), 307–322.

Kessler, G. (2015). Using technology to teach ESL readers & writers. In N. Evans, N. Anderson & B. Eggington (Eds.), *ESL readers and writers in higher education: Understanding challenges, providing support* (pp. 214–231). Routledge: London & New York.

Kessler, G., & Bikowski, D. (2011). The influence of SLA training in curricular design among teachers in preparation. *CALICO Journal, 28*(2), 522–545.

Kessler, G., & Plakans, L. (2008). Does teachers' confidence with CALL equal innovative and integrated use? *Computer Assisted Language Learning, 21*(3), 269–282.

Kolaitis, M., Mahoney, M., Pomann, H., & Hubbard, P. (2006) Training ourselves to train our students for CALL. In P. Hubbard & M. Levy (Eds.), *Teacher education in CALL* (pp. 317–332). Amsterdam: John Benjamins.

Levy, M., & Hubbard, P. (2005). Why call CALL "CALL"? *Computer Assisted Language Learning, 18*(3), 143–149.

Levy, M., & Stockwell, G. (2006). *CALL dimensions: Options and issues in computer-assisted language learning.* Mahwah, NJ: Lawrence Erlbaum Associates.

Appendix A

Course syllabus

Computers for language teaching 1 (Linguistics 4510/5510)

Greg Kessler
Gordy 017D
kessler@ohio.edu
593–2748

Office: Tues 1.00–3.00 pm
Gordy 015
Tue 3.05–6.00 pm

Course description

This is a course introducing the use of computer-assisted language learning (CALL). During this course we will explore the background of CALL as well as current trends in the field. We will learn to evaluate software, Internet materials and other components of CALL implementation. We will learn to use some software that is relevant to the creation of CALL materials. There will also be extensive discussion and practice on these topics through exercises in class. Each topic will also involve an extensive investigation into pedagogical approaches and implications.

Required text

None (as provided on Course Moodle: http://call.ohio.edu/moodle20/course/view.php?id=549)
Goals:
By the end of this course, students will be able to:

- Identify common and potential issues regarding CALL-related decision making
- Create effective CALL materials
- Collect and archive CALL materials
- Understand current approaches to CALL implementation
- Demonstrate the ability to introduce software for students
- Demonstrate the ability to evaluate software
- Demonstrate the ability to use a course management system (CMS)
- Demonstrate proficiency with the following software:
    - Hot Potatoes
    - Wikis
    - Blogs
    - Google Documents
    - Microsoft Office
    - Various Multimedia Software, possibly including:
      iMovie Audacity Wiretap

Project

The class will divide into groups and each group will select/create a target student population and design a sample set of materials (approximately a week of lessons) to meet that group's needs. Projects will include description of the materials in terms of content, level, type of technology used and relationship to the context of use. Considerations and issues faced during the decision-making process will also be addressed. Such decisions should be included in the final document. The group will present the materials and brief report of their creation and selection (three to five pages) during the last week of the quarter.

Discussion leading

Each student will be assigned a portion of the textbook (individually or as a group) on which they will lead a group discussion. These discussions will serve as the core of this class. These should be intended to involve all members of the class, not to serve as a formal presentation. Each discussion should involve a brief introduction to the article followed by a series of activities, hands-on practice or questions that support the article.

Collaborative midterm

During week ten, we collaboratively review the topics, concepts, tools and other issues addressed in the course up to that point. We co-construct questions covering these and the following week we take a collaborative exam.

Research paper (graduate students only)

Graduate students will be required to also write a five to seven page paper addressing an area of CALL theory, methodology or practice. These will be due at the end of week eight. All topics should be determined no later than Thursday of week five and cleared with me. I can offer suggestions for those who have no idea what to explore.

Evaluation

There will be four different kinds of evaluation: participation, discussion, leading and final projects. If it is necessary there may be occasional quizzes to review important information.

A	94–100	B–	80–82	Project	500
A–	91–93	C+	77–79	Leading class discussion	200
B+	87–90	C	73–76	Class participation	200

B	83–86	C–	70–73	Collaborative midterm	500
				Other homework/quizzes	100
				Exploratory paper (5510)	500
				Total points (4510)	1500
				Total points (5510)	2000

Tentative weekly overview

Week one

- Introduction to course, schedule, materials, expectations, course Moodle and the like.
- Introduction to the LRC (Prezi)
- Introduction to CALL (Prezi)
- Mac versus PC introduction
- Hot Potatoes, JMix and post to Moodle
- Course management systems (Blackboard and Moodle)

Homework for week two: 'Introduction: Foundations for teaching and learning' by Egbert & Hanson-Smith

Week two

- MS Office and language teaching
- Self access and autonomy (Prezi)
- Hot Potatoes, JQuiz, JMatch and post to Moodle
- Watch 'TED Talks: Sir Ken Robinson: Bring on the learning revolution!'
- Group discussion of 'Introduction: Foundations for teaching and learning'

Homework for week three: 'The future is now' by Price

Week three

- Mobile-assisted language learning (Prezi)
- Creating multimedia: iMovie
- Hot Potatoes, JCross, JCloze and post to Moodle
- Watch 'KFLC 2012 keynote by Julie Sykes: Digital games and language learning: Bridging the distance'
- Group discussion of 'The future is now'

Homework for week four: 'Theory and research: Language learning strategies' Egbert & Hanson-Smith

Week four

- New tools for teaching writing-as a foundation for other skills (Prezi)
- Google Suite and language teaching
- Watch 'CALICO 2011 keynote by Bryan Smith'
- Group discussion of 'Theory and research: Language learning strategies'

Homework for week five 'Collaborative language learning in co-constructed participatory culture.'

Week five

- CALL trends – gaming
- Watch 'Clay Shirky on cognitive surplus'
- Homework for week six: 'Hubbard, P. (2010). General introduction: *Computer assisted language learning: Critical concepts in Linguistics*.'
- Group discussion of 'Collaborative language learning in co-constructed participatory culture'
- Graduate students' paper topics due

Week six

- Collaboration & language learning in a world of ubiquitous computing
- ARIS games
- Hot Potatoes, JCross and post to Moodle
- Group discussion of 'Hubbard, P. (2010). General introduction: *Computer assisted language learning: Critical concepts in linguistics*.'
- Watch 'The future of learning and equality in a digital world'
- Homework for week seven: Fanfiction practices in ESL writing classrooms'

Week seven

- Video conferencing
- Wikis, blogs and CMC, What's next?
- Cool tools for schools
- Watch 'TED Talks: Gel: Gotta share!'
- Group discussion of 'Fanfiction Practices in ESL Writing Classrooms'
- Homework for week eight: 'SCMC for SLA: A research synthesis'

Week eight

- Geocaching
- Audio and video tools
- Group discussion of 'SCMC for SLA: A research synthesis'
- Watch 'TED Talks: Richard Baraniuk on open-source learning'
- Homework for week nine: 'Learner training for effective use of CALL' by Hubbard

Week nine

- Podcasting and audio recording
- iTunes U
- Evaluating software
- Watch 'IATEFL 2012 keynote by Steve Thorne: Awareness, appropriacy, and living language use'
- Group discussion of 'Learner training for effective use of CALL'
- Homework for week ten: 'TED Talks: Tim Berners-Lee: The year open data went worldwide'

Week ten

- Comic life
- Collaborative midterm construction
- Group discussion of 'TED Talks: Tim Berners-Lee: The year open data went worldwide'
- Homework for week eleven: Study for midterm

Week eleven

- Collaborative midterm exam
- Homework for week twelve: 'Theory and research: Investigating authenticity' by Chapelle and Liu (in Moodle)

Week twelve

- Material and lesson evaluation
- Clickers/response systems
- Watch 'TED talks by John Hockenberry: We are all designers'
- Group discussion of 'Theory and research: Investigating authenticity'

Homework for week thirteen: 'TED Talks: Nicholas Christakis: The hidden influence of social networks

Week thirteen

- The 'social' in language learning
- Group discussion of 'TED Talks: Nicholas Christakis: The hidden influence of social networks'
- Group project work
- Homework for week fourteen: 'Web 2.0, synthetic immersive environments, and the future of language education'

Week fourteen

- The future
- Group project work
- Group discussion of 'Web 2.0, synthetic immersive environments, and the future of language education'

Fri, 5:00pm: Papers due for graduate students

Week fifteen

- Presentation of final projects

Appendix B

Curricular Project Evaluation Rubric

CALL Project Presentation Evaluation **Group:** **Topic:**

Background

What is the main purpose of the course?
Who are the students and teachers?
How are students' needs diagnosed?
Where is the school located?
How does the course fit into the larger scheme of a programme of courses, or department or university, etc.?

Course CALL Materials (*rank this project according to the following criteria and provide examples*).

What are some technology tools that are utilized?

These tools are integrated well

1--------2--------3--------4--------5--------6--------7--------8--------9--------10

Comments:

These tools are explained well

1--------2--------3--------4--------5--------6--------7--------8--------9--------10

Comments:

These tools are used appropriately

1--------2--------3--------4--------5--------6--------7--------8--------9--------10

Comments:

Materials function as expected

1--------2--------3--------4--------5--------6--------7--------8--------9--------10

Comments:

Materials are aesthetically appealing

1--------2--------3--------4--------5--------6--------7--------8--------9--------10

Comments:

Materials are useful for students

1--------2--------3--------4--------5--------6--------7--------8--------9--------10

Comments:

Materials are innovative

1--------2--------3--------4--------5--------6--------7--------8--------9--------10

Comments:

Learner autonomy is promoted

1--------2--------3--------4--------5--------6--------7--------8--------9--------10

Comments:

Learner interaction is promoted

1--------2--------3--------4--------5--------6--------7--------8--------9--------10

Comments:

Negotiation of meaning is promoted

1--------2--------3--------4--------5--------6--------7--------8--------9--------10

Comments:

Authentic language use is promoted

1--------2--------3--------4--------5--------6--------7--------8--------9--------10

Comments:

What is one strength of this project?

What is one weakness of this project?

9

Teacher Training with CALL Online (Distance)

A Project- and Standards-Based Approach

Christine Bauer-Ramazani
Saint Michael's College, USA

Introduction

The CALL Online course for teacher trainees at Saint Michael's College has been taught full distance since 2000 and has trained around 150 native and non-native English speakers from around the world in the strategies of integrating technology inside and outside the classroom. The approach and methodology that has been the foundation of its success has remained the same since the first delivery of the CALL course in an online format in January 2000 and its face-to-face version in the late 1990s. The pillars of the course continue to be the integration of technology into teaching and learning through project-based learning (PBL), interaction, collaboration and task-based assessment (Bauer-Ramazani, 2006). However, since the establishment of standards for the use of technology in teaching in 2008 (ISTE, TESOL Technology Standards Framework), the course components have also been aligned with these standards. When the course was migrated from face-to-face to online/distance format, design and delivery features became increasingly important to ensure the continued success of the course. This chapter discusses these elements as well as the content and pedagogical principles of the course, review its distinctive features and alignment with CALL standards, address issues and challenges of teaching CALL Online and indicate future directions.

Context

Since its inception in the early 1990s, the CALL course at Saint Michael's College has been part of the teacher training programme in the Master of Arts in Teaching of English to Speakers of Other Languages (MATESOL) programme. As an elective, semester-based course throughout these years, it has enjoyed a steady stream of enrollment, both from within the on-campus MATESOL group of students as well as those teaching abroad and continuing their studies online. Additionally, teachers in need of CALL training would find the CALL demo site on the web (Bauer-Ramazani, 2000) and register for the course through Saint Michael's College. Due to the need for technology training with particular emphasis on language learning by current teachers or Master's degree candidates in education, the course has been cross-listed with the Master of Education programme at Saint Michael's College for quite some time. For several years the number of teaching/credit hours for the course has varied between three and four. In particular, it was popular as an intensive five-week online/distance summer course that attracted K-12 teachers and Master's degree candidates in Education as a way to fulfill course requirements in a short amount of time. As the needs of the MATESOL programme changed, in spring of 2014 it was again offered as a three-credit course but as part of the new MATESOL: OnLine + OnCampus programme at Saint Michael's College, where students can take four courses online, that is, full-distance, to complete the Master's in TESOL in as little as fourteen months by spending two summers on campus in Vermont and taking the remaining courses online. Since 2000, the course has been delivered through a learning management system (LMS), currently Canvas, which allows quick access by mobile devices and features integrated collaboration tools (e.g., Google Docs).

CALL Online fulfilling a need for training in technology

Students taking the CALL Online course come from varied backgrounds and experience in teaching and/or technology – from no teaching experience and little knowledge of technology to those that are currently teaching (K-12, adult education or intensive English programmes in higher education) and using technology for teaching but would like to expand their skills and knowledge about when to use technology, what technology to use and how to use it appropriately. Regarding the participants' educational backgrounds, most are MA candidates, but some hold a PhD or are working on a Bachelor's degree in TESOL as a special major. To address these varied needs, the course takes a PBL approach and not only discusses, but also very importantly, models the when, what and how of using technology in and outside the classroom to support all areas of language instruction.

Course description

Content of CALL Online

Although projects and technology tools have changed over the years – from multimedia to website construction to WebQuest creation to web templates to a portfolio wiki site, the current course description of GSL520/GED565: Computer-Assisted Language Learning expresses the focus and approach of the course; neither the focus nor the approach has changed dramatically over the years.

Course Description:

> Participants learn how to incorporate computer and mobile technology into flipped classroom lessons that enhance the skills of English language learners (K-12, adult) through project-based activities, including newsletters, animated slide shows, and free web-based multimedia and assessment tools. Participants construct an interactive/collaborative portfolio web space (wiki) for teaching and learning, review current research and follow the professional dialogue about technology in the classroom. They discuss the effectiveness of technological media through peer reviews and critical evaluation of web sites and/or courseware.

Learning outcomes and standards in CALL Online

CALL Online participants are expected to integrate the learned technologies into their specific teaching and learning environments (ESL, EFL, foreign language, technology in education). In particular, the learning outcomes expect CALL Online participants to:

1. establish an interactive and collaborative online learning community by using computer-mediated communication (CMC) tools, including a learning management system (computer-mediated communication literacy);
2. demonstrate their understanding of the history, theory, and research of CALL;

3. demonstrate competence in the use of computers and mobile devices as well as their applications for teaching, in particular language teaching (digital literacy);
4. author instructional materials for their target learners that incorporate applications for computers and mobile devices for flipping the classroom, including multimedia, Internet resources, and web-based authoring tools (multimedia literacy);
5. evaluate online information, resources, and courseware critically (information literacy);
6. practice the learned technologies with their students by incorporating similar projects into their specific teaching and learning environments (ESL, EFL, foreign language, technology in education);
7. identify and use online resources for professional development.

The four 'electronic literacies' are adapted from Warschauer (2002) but additional expectations have been added to meet the needs of twenty-first-century teachers, as expressed in the ISTE Standards for Teachers (2008) and the TESOL Technology Standards Framework (2008). In addition, the 2016 ISTE Standards for Students have also been consulted. As the CALL Online course incorporates these standards in many respects, they are listed for ease of reference.

ISTE Standards for Teachers (ISTE, 2008):

1. Facilitate and inspire student learning and creativity
2. Design and develop digital age learning experiences and assessments
3. Model digital age work and learning
4. Promote and model digital citizenship and responsibility
5. Engage in professional growth and leadership

TESOL Standards for Teachers (TESOL Technology Standards Framework, 2008):

Goal 1: Language teachers acquire and maintain foundational knowledge and skills in technology for professional purposes.

Goal 2: Language teachers integrate pedagogical knowledge and skills with technology to enhance language teaching and learning.

Goal 3: Language teachers apply technology in record-keeping, feedback, and assessment.

Goal 4: Language teachers use technology to improve communication, collaboration, and efficiency.

To measure the learning outcomes in CALL Online the following instruments have been built into the course. They are discussed in the Features section below:

1. A Reading Discussion Forum with moderators
2. A Sharing What You Learned Discussion Forum with moderators
3. Interactive and collaborative tasks (peer reviews)
4. Hands-on projects
5. A collaborative web site review
6. A collaborative course materials review
7. A portfolio web space course project (wiki), which can function as a free learning management system (LMS)

Features and issues

Course delivery and pre-course start-up tasks

As the course is delivered fully online/distance, or DCALL, as Lamy (2013) refers to such courses, logistical set-up procedures need to be addressed before course participants can delve into the content. Thus, the goal is to have these start-up tasks completed prior to the course start date and to focus on content and discussions of content thereafter. In addition, as most course participants may not have had experience with online/distance courses and may have varying expectations, transparency of procedures, content and expectations is critical to the success of all participants in the course. This section discusses various aspects of course delivery, from pre-course preparations and logistics to course components and assessment.

Student needs assessment. Given the students' varied background and needs in terms of both teaching environment (current and future) as well as experience with technology, several types of needs assessments are taken prior to the start of the course. The purpose is twofold: (1) to assess the students' skills, familiarity and comfort level with technology and (2) to customize readings, projects, suggested links and discussion responses to the students' needs to the extent possible. Thus, students are first asked to complete a quick, multiple-choice online self-assessment (Community College of Philadelphia, n.d.) of their suitability to online learning, including questions regarding organizational skills, autonomous learning capability, monitoring progress, preferred learning styles, inclination to experiment with new things and more. Of those, organizational skills, including time management and autonomous learning capability are usually the strongest predictors of who will do well in CALL Online. Second, course participants are asked to complete a questionnaire about their contact information, current or future teaching environment and experience, career goal, computer/mobile device specifics, experience with various technological tools and applications and use of technology with students.

Getting started/Orientation. As many course participants have never taken an online/distance course, it is necessary to orient them to the logistics and expectations of such a course, including course access, the course schedule, required time-on-task, prerequisite skills (typing, computer, data/file management, Google Drive, usernames, etc.), software/hardware, reading materials, where/how to get help, course organization, course progression, attendance, interaction, video tutorials, a video on the goals of CALL Online as well as other videos about CALL. Course participants receive this information well ahead of the course start date. A vital element built into all orientation materials is the Terms of Agreement, familiar to consumers of electronic information, to ensure that course delivery and responsibilities have been communicated and understood.

Syllabus. The syllabus is also communicated to course participants prior to the course start date for similar reasons as outlined above. The most important elements on the syllabus include required subscriptions, interaction and projects and assessment criteria. As with the Getting Started/Orientation information, the students are required to submit their Terms of Agreement.

Required subscriptions. As part of their course start-up tasks, course participants are required to subscribe to professional communities of practice (CoPs) like Learning2gether (https://learning2gether.net/), CALL-related Google+ communities or an *Electronic Village Online* session (Hanson-Smith & Bauer-Ramazani, 2004) as well as free electronic publications like *T.H.E. Journal, TechLearning, EduWire, Faculty Focus, Free Technology for Teachers K-12 Blueprint.* The purpose of this assignment is to not only familiarize the course participants with the topics discussed by educators in the field of CALL, but also help them establish a network of professionals to use as a resource for their continued professional development in teaching and learning with technology (Hanson-Smith, 2006). This fulfills ISTE Standard 5 (ISTE, 2008) and Goal 4, Standard 2 of the Technology Standards for Teachers (TESOL Technology Standards Framework, 2008). Course participants follow the dialogue in the CoPs and post a reaction within the LMS. Later, course participants set up their own Pinterest, Scoop.It, Google+, Diigo and/or Twitter sites for curating, bookmarking, tagging and sharing important websites or tools for teaching and learning as well as follow well-recognized leaders in the field of CALL.

Course content

Goals of CALL Online. A video '*Goals of CALL Online*' on the Getting Started/ Orientation page of the course describes the course goal as follows:

> The goal of this course is to learn about strategies, applications, and tools that help teachers integrate technology into learning and teaching. Central to the philosophy of CALL and reverberating throughout my teaching with technology is this sentence: It's not about the tools; it's about using the tools to facilitate learning. Thus, technology is simply a tool, a means to an end, not an end in itself. It must be embedded into a pedagogical approach, including objectives, procedure and strategy (preparation, presentation, practice), assessment and follow-up.

This approach of embedding technology into pedagogy and content is anchored in the Technological Pedagogical Content Knowledge (TPCK, Mishra & Koehler, 2006; now also referred to as TPACK, Koehler, 2011) framework which discusses and illustrates 'the complex roles of, and interplay among, three main components of learning environments: content, pedagogy, and technology' (p. 1017). The content or subject matter in the CALL Online course relates to all areas of language learning with technology in English as a Second or Foreign Language (ESL/EFL), including the four skills of reading, writing, listening, speaking, as well as grammar, vocabulary and pronunciation. However, content extends far beyond these areas of language learning to include up-to-date research and insights into practices of language learning and teaching, such as mobile learning, flipped learning, gaming (gamification) and project-based learning. There are no lectures but content is presented and carefully scaffolded through videos, hands-on instructions and models that illustrate the integration of technology into teaching (Bauer-Ramazani, 2016a). The technology components include the tools, devices and applications that can be employed in the processes, practices or methods of teaching and learning ESL/EFL. Thus, these three components represent the anchors for the topics, readings and discussions, models as well as projects to be completed by the course participants in CALL Online.

Topics. The weekly topics in the CALL Online course examine a wide range of CALL applications in language learning and teaching (breadth) but the built-in projects provide depth (Hubbard, 2007) as well. They are distributed across the

Table 9.1 Alignment of content components in CALL Online with standards

Content components of CALL Online	**TESOL Technology Standards Framework**	**ISTE Standards**
1. Goals of the course; goals of the course project (a wiki as a portfolio and learning management system); definition of terms (CALL, blended learning, 21st-century technology skills); goals and history of CALL	Goal 1, Standard 3; Goal 4, Standards 1, 2, 3	Standards 1, 2, 3
2. Literacies (digital, computer-mediated communication, information, multimedia) – see learning outcomes above.	Goal 1, Standards 1, 2, 4; Goal 2, Standards 1, 3; Goal 3, Standard 1	Standards 2, 3, 4
3. Teaching writing online • Collaborating, revision, reviewing	Goal 4, Standard 3	Standards 1, 2, 3
4. Using presentation software for teaching and learning • Using pedagogically purposeful animation	Goal 1, Standard 1	Standards 1, 2
5. Strategies and tools for collaboration in an online environment • Leveraging Google Drive for collaborative learning and teaching	Goal 4, Standard 3	Standards 1, 2, 3
6. Using the Internet and mobile apps to support teaching and learning in language areas, with emphasis on reading, listening, speaking, writing, grammar, vocabulary, pronunciation	Goal 1, Standard 2; Goal 2, Standard 3; Goal 4, Standard 1	Standards 2, 3
7. Evaluating CALL resources and materials (websites, online courseware, apps)	Goal 3, Standards 1, 2, 3, 4	Standards 2, 5
8. Project-based learning and teaching • Identifying appropriate tools for learning and teaching • Flipping the classroom • BYOD (Bring Your Own Device)	Goal 1, Standard 3; Goal 2, Standard 3	Standards 1, 3
9. Using concordancing for teaching and learning	Goal 3, Standard 2	Standards 1, 2
10. Gaming (Gamification) in teaching and learning	Goal 1, Standard 3; Goal 2, Standard 1	Standards 1, 2
11. Authoring content to support teaching and learning in all language areas, with emphasis on reading, listening, speaking, writing, grammar, vocabulary, pronunciation	Goal 2, Standard 2	Standards 2, 3

Content components of CALL Online	TESOL Technology Standards Framework	ISTE Standards
12. Electronic assessment – formative and summative • Embedded web 2.0 tools for exercises, flashcards, quizzes and rubrics • Electronic gradebooks	Goal 3, Standards 1, 3; Goal 4, Standard 3	Standard 2
13. Communities of practice (CoPs): Online professional development resources and strategies to stay on the cutting edge of developments in TESOL and CALL	Goal 1, Standard 3; Goal 2, Standards 2, 4; Goal 4, Standards 1, 2	Standard 5

fifteen weeks of the course. Table 9.1 shows alignment of topics with the TESOL Technology Standards Framework (2008) and the ISTE Standards for Teachers (2008).

Course design and components. The major components of CALL Online are found within the LMS of Canvas and can be accessed by the course participants on computers or mobile devices (See Figure 9.1): Home, Syllabus, Modules, Announcements, Discussions, Assignments, Conferences, Grades, Files and Collaborations.

The course design is based on a modular approach, with each week representing one course module. Typically, weeks begin on Monday and end on Sunday at midnight. Dates for the week, including any holidays, are indicated in the weekly module. In order to facilitate navigation by the online course participants, all modules are consistent in components, titles, as well as format and layout.

Each module consists of two content pages:

1. the weekly Tasks
2. the weekly Reading Assignments

as well as five discussion forums:

1. Reading Selections (Participants indicate their chosen articles.)
2. Reading Discussion Forum: Summaries/Reactions/Interaction
3. Sharing What You Learned Discussion Forum (including twice a semester: Reaction to a Posting in a professional CoP that the participants have subscribed to as part of their requirements)
4. The Professor's Office
5. Virtual Café for Students

Figure 9.1 Course components.

See Figure 9.2 for a representative example of a course module.

The dates next to the three discussion forums refer to the due date for the discussions in each as well as the number of weekly points to be earned for grading.

Interaction

Interaction is the lifeblood of any online/distance course. In order for the students and the course to be successful, participants need to be involved in an ongoing dialogue. Interaction is the main ingredient in establishing and maintaining a vibrant online knowledge and learning community and is found in several course components:

1. The discussion forums (Reading Discussion Forum, Sharing What You Learned Discussion Forum, The Professor's Office, Virtual Café for Students)
2. Moderating the discussions

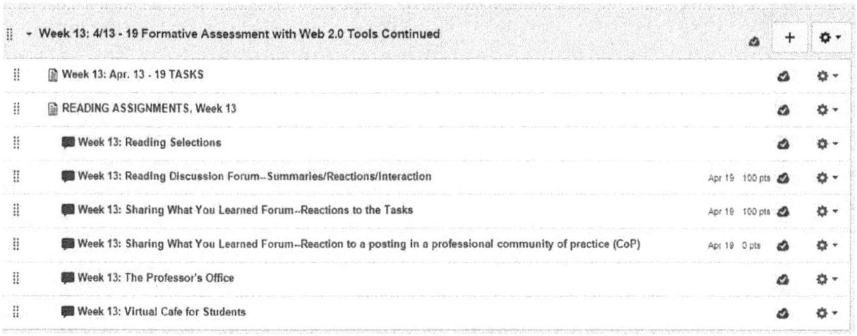

Figure 9.2 A weekly course module.

In order to guide interaction in all course components, the instructor's approach can best be described as 'directed facilitation', a term introduced by Shea, Li, and Pickett (2006). These authors' study revealed that 'a strong and active presence on the part of the instructor – one in which she or he actively guides and orchestrates the discourse – is related both to students' sense of connectedness and learning' (p. 185). In CALL Online, course participants establish an online knowledge and learning community in which it is safe to post reflections, questions, requests for help, agreements, constructive criticism, humour, appreciation of support – all around shared educational objectives and the co-construction of meaning in an environment where all participants mentor each other.

Readings and the Reading Discussion Forum. The interplay of the three components of the TPACK framework (Koehler, 2011) – content, pedagogy, technology – is reflected in the selection of readings representing the current knowledge, research and pedagogy in the field of CALL. No main textbook is required; instead, almost 500 book chapters and articles from CALL journals (*Computer-Assisted Language Learning, CALICO, ReCall, Language Learning & Technology, System*) and a variety of journals and magazines focusing on technology in education are grouped into various topics that support the topic of each week. Thus, readings include articles on research and practice with technology in a variety of teaching environments, such as ESL or EFL in higher education, K-12, adult education or teacher training. Chapters in several electronic resources are highlighted, including the most recent issue of the New Media Consortium (NMC)'s *New Horizon Report: Higher Education Edition*, the NMC *New Horizon Report K-12 Edition* and current e-texts, such as Thomas, Reinders, and Warschauer (2013) as well as Motteram (2013). Texts are frequently changed to retain currency, and readings are updated each semester. Course participants are required to select, read and discuss at least one article per week. The decision to use this approach to readings was made in order to keep course participants on the cutting edge of new developments in CALL and be more able to respond to the speed of innovation in technology, devices and applications as well as the appearance of new trends in pedagogical approaches to technology. Thus, course participants encounter up-to-date research, technologies and teaching techniques that allow them to customize their readings to their own current or future teaching environment, a critical criterion in reaching all students.

The jigsaw reading strategy and summaries/reactions. In order to address the variety of readings course participants are instructed to use a jigsaw strategy: students read and post summaries of different chapters/articles, thus covering a range of topics. The summaries of the articles should clarify the main points of the articles and allow clear understanding for someone who has not read the article. Each week, course participants post a summary, followed by a reaction. The choices of articles are specified in the Reading Selections Forum each week in order to avoid duplication. In addition, course participants are required to post two substantive interactive comments in response to summaries/reactions posted by others. This jigsaw strategy has been effective as it allows for lively discussions of cutting-edge applications of technology in CALL and expands the students' horizon beyond that of the chapter or article they summarized.

In the reaction, students are asked to discuss the arguments presented, point out any strengths and possible limitations or weaknesses and discuss applications of the concepts to their teaching environment. Any crossovers from other theories or disciplines should be addressed. In general, substantive reactions include possibilities for using the ideas or conclusions in the typical classroom.

Assessment of discussions. Posts by the course participants in the Reading Discussion Forum are assessed according to the criteria outlined above, the number and quality of summaries/reactions, as well as the number and substance of interactive comments in response to other posts. This assessment occurs after discussions have closed for the week through a primary-trait rubric designed by the instructor and accompanying each assignment. The criteria include

- Completion of summary and reaction as required
- Identification and discussion of salient points in the summary
- Application of principles discussed in the reading to a teaching and learning environment
- The number and timeliness of substantive responses to the posts of other course participants.

Tasks and the Sharing What You Learned Discussion Forum. The tasks chosen for the construction of technological pedagogical content knowledge (Mishra & Koehler, 2006) provide the technical scaffolding, the pedagogical context and the pedagogical modeling for larger CALL projects that span two weeks or more. Tasks can be subsumed under Goal 2 of the TESOL Standards for Language Teachers (TESOL Technology Standards Framework, 2008): 'Language teachers integrate pedagogical knowledge and skills with technology to enhance language teaching and learning' (p. 32). The approach taken to the weekly tasks follows a traditional pedagogical paradigm that includes:

1. The learning outcome expected by the end of the week
2. Background readings discussing the task and/or particular technology related to the task
3. An introduction/presentation of the task
4. Practice through links to hands-on tutorials and reviews of models or samples contributed by previous course participants
5. Performance through reflections on the tasks in the Sharing What You Learned Forum, posting of first drafts, peer reviews and revisions
6. Assessment through a rubric posted for each task

For a sample task, see Figure 9.3.

In addition, students learn about, review and are expected to incorporate a variety of digital resources available for instructional use through a compendium of links (Bauer-Ramazani, 1997–2017) and mobile apps, and by sharing resources with each other. All are expected to support teaching and learning in the areas of language learning, with emphasis on reading, listening, speaking, writing, grammar, vocabulary and pronunciation. Tasks also include opportunities to experiment with more recent approaches and technologies, such as flipping the classroom, Bring Your Own Device (BYOD) and mobile apps. They are followed by a reaction in the Sharing What You Learned Forum, which must include a discussion of the effectiveness of the presented tool or technology in the language classroom. In addition, course participants are expected to post a minimum of three substantive interactive comments in response to their peers' postings. A rubric measures the task reactions as well as the interaction of participants according to these criteria:

- Completion of tasks as required
- Substantive discussion of salient points
- Incorporation of concepts and principles from the readings and course resources

TASKS WEEK 6

This week's learning focus is on strategies for collaboration in an online environment for the purpose of reviewing and critically evaluating Web sites. In addition, we will learn more about leveraging Google Drive for collaborative learning and teaching.

Learning outcomes for this week:

1. **Strategies and tools for collaboration in an online environment**
2. **Reviewing and critically evaluating Web sites**
3. **Peer reviews of PowerPoint lessons**
4. Constructing the Web space course project (Wiki)--organizing files and pages into folders

Review/Click on each Task separately and complete the instructions. After completing each task, return to this page. Feel free to skip information that you already know or have completed earlier.

In this section you will experience using the Internet and/or mobile technology for real-time (synchronous) communication in order to carry out a group task. Then you will visit some sample Internet sites for content and critical evaluation. The collaborative review is a two-week project.

Task 1: Teamwork (collaborative/interactive task)--Please note the timelines below!

Objective/expected outcome: In this task you will be working in teams (see team assignments below) to choose web sites to visit and to write a team response, which will be due March 1. Your assignment this week is to agree on **three** sites from the different categories in Task 2, visit them, try out the offered applications (Web pages, audio/video, etc.), hold some group discussions, and begin identifying criteria of Web site evaluation. **By Wednesday, 4:00 US EDT**, send me an e-mail message **with your team's choices.**

Strategies and tools for collaboration on a project in an online environment

1. Figuring out availability dates/times for team members: Try Doodle .
2. **Computer-Mediated Communication (CMC) alternatives to meet the Wednesday deadline:**

Figure 9.3 Sample task.

- Application to a teaching and learning environment
- Number and timeliness of substantive responses to other participants'

Assessments are posted, along with comments, after the week's discussions have closed.

Through the process of scaffolded tasks, discussions and problem-solving, course participants are expected to become autonomous learners by the end of the course. The goal of training autonomous CALL teachers and self-directed learning is indeed a critical component of CALL, as has been emphasized by Warschauer (2002), Robb (2006), Reinders and Hubbard (2013) as well as Reinders and White (2016).

Moderating the discussions. In order to engage the learners in the weekly discussions and create a vibrant knowledge building online community, course participants moderate the discussions in the two forums. Each forum has a weekly Starter and Wrapper as co-moderators for the discussions. Being a moderator means 'leading the discussion.' Starters are expected to post critical thinking questions about readings and tasks, while wrappers sum up the contributions to the discussion. Thus, the moderators carry the bulk of interaction each week.

The contributions by the moderators are assessed at the end of the week with a primary-trait rubric that measures:

- the number, timeliness and substance of questions posted by the Starter
- the co-moderator's ongoing interaction with the class
- the substance, completeness and timeliness of the discussions posted by the Wrapper.

This regimen of moderating threaded discussions has been effectively used in CALL Online for a number of years and follows recommendations for encouraging learner participation in online discussion forums (Craig, 2015; Thormann, 2009, 2014).

The Professor's Office and the Virtual Café for Students. Two additional discussion forums are designed for interaction with the professor and participants to interact among themselves. The Professor's Office tends to be more heavily used at the beginning of the course to ask questions, get clarification, indicate problems or discuss issues encountered related to course resources or tasks. This forum is checked by the instructor several times a day and posts are visible to all participants. By Week 4 or 5, course participants seem to have settled into a routine, are familiar with expectations and procedures, and only occasionally utilize the Professor's Office. This may indicate that they have become more autonomous learners and found other means of answering their questions, for example, by using the Help function in a specific application or environment.

Web conferences. Web conferences or synchronous, real-time chats are an important interactive component in CALL Online held every few weeks. While real-time chats are difficult to arrange across time zones on several continents, needs arise to reconnect with all course participants around housekeeping issues, questions, problems or clarifications. In addition, tools, content and pedagogy are discussed. An agenda outlines content questions regarding the weekly topic for the participants to discuss in breakout rooms (if available) or whole class mode. The last web conference of the semester focuses on the presentation and review of the course projects, the wikis, as a portfolio of learning and teaching. Thus, the web conference application must allow for text chat, document presentation, desktop sharing and URL posting for presentations.

Projects

While interaction is the lifeblood of CALL Online and allows the instructor to monitor the students' progress in understanding the concepts and principles taught, the project components to be completed by course participants provide the instructor with further means of assessment. Projects vary in length and type and include:

1. an individual course project (fifteen weeks) – a portfolio web space (wiki) for learning and teaching;
2. individual projects that incorporate productivity tools, digital age learning experiences, and assessments – a CALL newsletter, a CALL lesson presentation, four formative shareable assessment tools (exercise, quiz, flashcards, rubric, online gradebook);
3. interactive and collaborative projects – five peer reviews on the projects above;
4. collaborative projects (groups of three and two, respectively) – reviews of websites and online instructional materials, including mobile apps.

All projects are carefully scaffolded: They state expected outcomes with a list of specific components (technological and pedagogical) to be incorporated and provide links to support materials (e.g., online instructions in text or video). Very importantly, a required task is for course participants to review and comment on models provided by previous CALL students, professional resources or the instructor. Assessment is conducted with the use of rubrics that incorporate the traits outlined in the learning outcome. An example is the CALL Presentation Lesson rubric (Bauer-Ramazani, 2016b). All projects described are to be incorporated into the wiki designed and constructed by the course participants.

As CALL Online is anchored in a project-based learning (PBL) approach (Buck Institute of Education, 2015a, 2015b), the projects constructed by course participants are expected to illustrate how they would teach their chosen topic to a target audience while incorporating a particular technology tool or application. In other words, the students learn how to 'use their knowledge of subject matter, teaching and learning, and technology to facilitate experiences that advance student learning, creativity, and innovation' (ISTE Standards for Teachers, Standard 1, 2008) and 'coherently integrate technology into their pedagogical approaches' (TESOL Standards for Teachers, Goal 2, Standard 2, p. 32). Thus, projects are authentic in that they require course participants to configure outcomes based on the needs of learners and teaching situations following the traditional paradigm of a lesson. It is hoped that this intentionally scaffolded integration of authentic and pedagogically driven projects will provide a more situation- and education-based approach to CALL teacher training and mitigate some of the barriers to technology use (Egbert, Paulus, & Nakamichi, 2002; Motteram, Slaouti, & Onat-Stelma, 2013).

The portfolio web space (wiki) for teaching and learning. The current semester-long course project is a wiki for ubiquitous teaching and learning. It is conceived as a type of free learning management system (LMS) that serves a dual purpose: (1) it functions as a portfolio of the course participants' work in the CALL course and as a technology tool for communication and collaboration. However, the CALL Online wiki project is expected to extend far beyond the course; (2) thus, the wiki project instructs course participants in the design and use of wikis for their own teaching context. In other words, course participants learn how to customize this web space for their own courses and for their students as learning and collaboration spaces. To this end, course participants build their LMS using the free basic educational wiki of PBworks (http://www.pbworks.com/) for current and future use anywhere in the world and without being limited to the resources provided (or not provided) by an institution they are affiliated with. This space can be completely private or accessed by those with a registered account.

Collaborative projects. These projects have probably been enjoyed the most by course participants over the years. With considerable scaffolding course participants conduct a critical analysis of several websites and instructional materials (online or mobile apps) in collaboration with other course participants located in different parts of the world. To facilitate collaborations across time and space they learn to select and employ the most appropriate from a variety of collaborative tools, such as Google Drive, web conferencing, wiki pages, Skype, Google Hangout, text messaging and more. Sites and instructional materials are reviewed based on criteria of evaluation and include a discussion of alignment with needs and abilities of the learners, pedagogical applications, limitations, recommendations and appropriate citations. One reason for the continued success of these collaborative projects may lie in the approach to learning described as the social construction of knowledge (Vygotsky, 1978) and constructionism or 'learning-by-making' (Papert & Harel, 1991), where learning is a social act and meaning is co-constructed by the learners in a meaningful context.

The pedagogical framework of CALL Online

A video recording posted at the end of the CALL Online course summarizes what has been taught as the best practices in CALL, reminding course participants of the goals of CALL – the need for transferring what they learned about

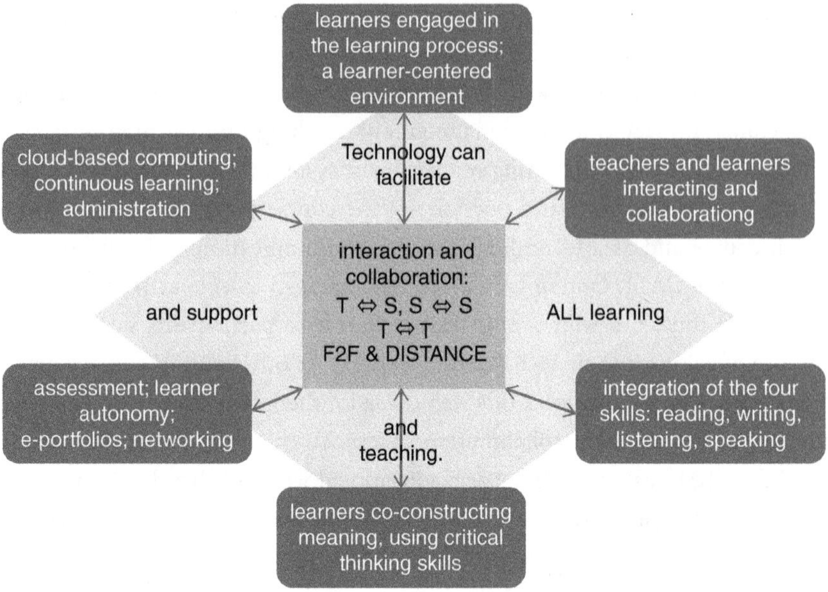

Figure 9.4 Pedagogical framework of teacher training in CALL.

the integration of technology to their learners, engaging them in interaction, collaboration and co-construction of meaning, guiding them towards autonomous learning with technology and continuing the learning process themselves. The pedagogical framework of teacher training in Figure 9.4 is adapted from the Conditions for Optimal Language Learning Environments (Egbert, Hanson-Smith, & Chao, 2007).

Issues in CALL Online

Issues in CALL Online have presented themselves in the form of challenges, many of them inherent in the nature of distance courses, others due to the fast-paced changes in technology.

Communication and collaboration. Working across different continents and time zones is challenging for learners and teachers. Both need to take distance-related issues into consideration, for example due dates and times on interactive and collaborative projects. Files must be uploaded in time for reviewers to make comments. Course participants may have to be reminded to be mindful of the impact of time zones on collaborative work. In some cases synchronous or real-time communication may not be possible, thus ruling out tools like Skype,

Google Hangout, web conferencing and real-time Google Drive, having students turn to asynchronous tools like email, Google Drive, texting, wikis and the like. However, working across distances constitutes twenty-first-century digital citizenship and is expected in the global economy, thus providing authenticity to such tasks and contexts.

Changes in content focus. In order to stay up-to-date with current trends in pedagogy and technology education in language learning, constant changes and adaptations in readings, instructional materials, projects and tools are necessary, sometimes every semester. Learning outcomes have to reflect these changes.

Rapid changes in technology. Links to tools, training documents, topic-related readings, as well as instructional materials frequently go dead, requiring searches for replacements and sometimes major adaptation of a project. This work is typically more extensive and time-consuming for CALL Online than other content courses, distance or face-to-face.

Availability of up-to-date textbooks appropriate for the goals of CALL Online. Textbooks in CALL research and pedagogy become quickly outdated. The ideal textbook for CALL Online would include standards-based methodology for CALL, project-based teaching and learning, up-to-date technology tools as well as models of the incorporation of technology in teaching and learning.

Changes in learning management systems, increasing workload. The recent migration from one LMS to another at Saint Michael's College caused extensive and time-consuming adjustments to be made to the design and structure of CALL Online to ensure seamless delivery and full functionality of all features previously used to enhance interactivity and collaboration. Such adjustments are more extensive for distance courses than for face-to-face courses, requiring significant time commitments by the instructor without compensation. It is necessary to monitor constantly for potential issues (e.g., links, upload/download assignments, peer review assignments), and be ready to find on-the-spot workaround solutions.

Future directions

CALL Online as a required course

CALL Online has been an elective course at Saint Michael's College and it is unlikely that this will change in the future, given the structure of the programme and the division of credits within it. However, for all students in the Online Strand option, the course is one of the four courses offered at a distance, thus making the course a requirement. With the trajectory of enrollment in online/distance courses at private non-profit four-year institutions like Saint Michael's College increasing faster than overall higher education enrollments and particularly in private non-profit four-year institutions (Allen & Seaman, 2015), it is expected that more students will be taking CALL Online during their off-campus semester, thus contributing to an increase in teacher education and competence in CALL in accordance with CALL standards. Although these Online-Strand students typically are higher users of technology, they need to become versed in the pedagogical affordances of technology for language learning.

Increased desire for learning about principles of online course design

Questions about a course in the principles of online course design for English language learning have occasionally been raised by participants in CALL Online. While TESOL has offered such courses as part of its Principles and Practices of Online Teaching Certificate Program, it is expected that such requests will become more frequent.

Increase in the widespread use of social technologies and mobile devices potentially impacting course design

In response to the continued increase in the use of social technologies and mobile devices by students, it is hoped that teachers will increasingly respond to their ubiquity and learn to harness their capabilities for language learning. It is expected that in the near future CALL Online will incorporate an even heavier focus on individual and collaborative projects involving the increased use of social technologies and mobile devices for in- and out-of-class activities and networking, such as those described by Dudeney and Hockly (2014) and Berge and Muilenburg (2013), thus potentially impacting course design. However, similar to observations made by Steel and Levy (2013), participants in CALL Online have tended to use social technologies for activities unrelated to class. It remains to be seen if they will employ the affordances of these social technologies for learning and teaching, whether in the classroom or outside of it. Echoing Reinders and White (2016), more empirical studies are needed on the added pedagogical value of such technologies.

A wish-list: Enticing current teachers to adopt CALL and rewarding CALL practices

While current or future CALL teachers may have recognized the need to be adequately prepared in the effective use of technology in education, this may not be the case for teachers in general. Teachers who do not use technology for teaching and learning often seem to lack curiosity to find out more about the affordances of various technology tools or their pedagogical applications in the classroom. They also find it more time-consuming to learn about the affordances of various types of technology and identify appropriate ways to integrate it into the classroom, so they may avoid doing so (Hubbard, 2007; Kessler, 2006). Furthermore, they may be afraid that the students know more than the teachers do and do not want to appear incompetent, so they avoid using appropriate technology. Thus, ways need to be found to entice more currently practicing language teachers to adopt CALL and technology-integrated teaching and learning and rewards for those that do.

Such solutions make it incumbent upon institutions to require the use of CALL methodology and make the integration of technology into teaching and learning a goal or standard within the MATESOL curriculum. Workshops and mentoring in this methodology are necessary components of professional development. In accordance with Kessler's (2006) research, an incentive and rewards structure should be built in order for this solution to become effective strategy. Furthermore, the 4Es model by Son, Robb, Hubbard, Stevens and Seburn (2015), calling teachers to explore, engage, evaluate and enhance, offers valuable strategies for self-directed professional development (SDPD) in CALL environments. These strategies, indeed, represent those followed by the author of this chapter in her own SDPD and the principles and practices of the CALL Online course described here in leading course participants to autonomous and successful integration of technology in their own learning and teaching, described as 'teacher autonomy' by Reinders and White (2016, p. 146).

References

Allen, I., & Seaman, J. (2015). Grade level: Tracking online education in the United States, 2014. *Online Learning Consortium*. Retrieved from http://onlinelearningconsortium.org/read/survey-reports-2014/

Bauer-Ramazani, C. (1997–2017). Christine's links to useful TESL/CALL web resources. Retrieved from http://academics.smcvt.edu/cbauer-ramazani/Links/useful_sites.htm

Bauer-Ramazani, C. (2006). Training CALL teachers online. In P. Hubbard & M. Levy (Eds.), *Teacher Education in CALL* (pp. 183–200). Amsterdam: John Benjamins.

Bauer-Ramazani, C. et al. (2016a). Flipped learning in TESOL: Definitions, approaches, and implementation. *TESOL Journal, 7*(2), 429–437.

Bauer-Ramazani, C. (2016b). CALL lesson presentation rubric. Retrieved from http://bit.ly/1FLCx8T

Berge, Z., & Muilenburg, L. (Eds.) (2013). *Handbook of mobile learning.* New York: Routledge.

Buck Institute of Education (2015a). What is project-based learning? Retrieved from http://bie.org/about/what_pbl

Buck Institute of Education (2015b). Why project-based learning (PBL)? Retrieved from http://bie.org/about/why_pbl

Community College of Philadelphia (n.d.). Self-Assessment. Retrieved from http://faculty.ccp.edu/faculty/msaks/ccpde/self_asmt.html

Craig, G. (2015, February 12). Evaluation discussion forums for undergraduate and graduate students. *Faculty Focus.* Retrieved from http://www.facultyfocus.com/articles/online-education/evaluating-discussion-forums-undergraduate-graduate-students/

Dudeney, G., & Hockly, N. (2014). *Going mobile: Teaching with hand-held devices.* Surrey, England: Delta.

Egbert, J., Hanson-Smith, E., & Chao, C. (2007). Introduction: Foundations for teaching and learning. In J. Egbert and E. Hanson-Smith (Eds.), *CALL environments: Research, practice, and critical issues* (2nd ed.). Alexandria, VA: TESOL.

Egbert, J., Paulus, T., & Nakamichi, Y. (2002). The impact of CALL instruction on classroom computer use: A foundation for rethinking technology in teacher education. *Language Learning & Technology, 6*(3), 108–126. Retrieved from http://llt.msu.edu/vol6num3/egbert/

Hanson-Smith, E. (2006). Communities of practice for pre- and in-service teacher education. In P. Hubbard & M. Levy (Eds.), *Teacher Education in CALL* (pp. 301–315). Amsterdam: John Benjamins.

Hanson-Smith, E., & Bauer-Ramazani, C. (2004). Professional development: The electronic village online of the TESOL CALL interest section. *TESL-EJ, 8*(2). Retrieved from http://tesl-ej.org/ej30/int.html

Hubbard, P. (2007). CALL and the future of language teacher education. *CALICO Journal, 25*(2), 175–188.

ISTE standards for teachers (2008). *International Society for Technology in Education.* Retrieved from http://www.iste.org/docs/pdfs/20-14_ISTE_Standards-T_PDF.pdf

ISTE standards for students (2016). In redefining learning in a technology-driven world (2016, June). *International Society for Technology in Education.* Retrieved from http://www.iste.org/standards/standards/for-students-2016

Johnson, L., Adams Becker, S., Estrada, V., & Freeman, A. (2015). *NMC Horizon Report: 2015 K-12 Edition.* Austin, TX: The New Media Consortium. Retrieved from http://cdn.nmc.org/media/2015-nmc-horizon-report-k12-EN.pdf

Johnson, L., Adams Becker, S., Cummins, M., Estrada, V., Freeman, A., & Hall, C. (2016). *NMC Horizon Report: 2016 Higher Education Edition.* Austin, Texas: The New Media Consortium. Retrieved from http://www.nmc.org/publication/nmc-horizon-report-2016-higher-education-edition/

Kessler, G. (2006). Assessing CALL teacher training. In P. Hubbard & M. Levy (Eds.), *Teacher education in CALL* (pp. 23–42). Amsterdam: John Benjamins.

Koehler, M. (2011). What is TPACK? *TPACK.org*. Retrieved from http://tpack.org/

Lamy, M.-N. (2013). Distance CALL online. In M. Thomas, H. Reinders, & M. Warschauer (Eds.), *Contemporary computer-assisted language learning* (pp. 141–158). London: Bloomsbury.

Mishra, P., & Koehler, M. (2006). Technological pedagogical content knowledge: A framework for teacher knowledge. *Teachers College Record, 108*(6), 1017–1054. Retrieved from http://punya.educ.msu.edu/publications/journal_articles/mishra-koehler-tcr2006.pdf

Motteram, G. (Ed.). (2013). *Innovations in learning technologies for English language teaching*. British Council: Teaching English. Retrieved from http://www.teachingenglish.org.uk/sites/teacheng/files/C607%20Information%20and%20Communication_WEB%20ONLY_FINAL.pdf

Motteram, G., Slaouti, D., & Onat-Stelma, Z. (2013). Second language teacher education for CALL: An alignment of practice and theory. In M. Thomas, H. Reinders, & M. Warschauer (Eds.), *Contemporary computer-assisted language learning* (pp. 55–71). London: Bloomsbury.

Papert, S., & Harel, I. (1991). *Constructionism*. New York: Ablex.

Reinders, H., & Hubbard, P. (2013). CALL and learner autonomy: Affordances and constraints. In M. Thomas, H. Reinders, & M. Warschauer (Eds.), *Contemporary computer-assisted language learning* (pp. 359–375). London: Bloomsbury.

Reinders, H., & White, C. (2016). 20 years of autonomy and technology: How far have we come and where to next? *Language Learning & Technology, 20*(2), 143–154. Retrieved from http://llt.msu.edu/issues/june2016/reinderswhite.pdf

Robb, T. (2006). Helping teachers to help themselves. In P. Hubbard & M. Levy (Eds.), *Teacher education in CALL* (pp. 335–347). Amsterdam: John Benjamins.

Shea, P., Li, C. S., & Pickett, A. (2006). A study of teaching presence and student sense of learning community in fully online and web-enhanced college courses. *Internet and Higher Education, 9*, 175–190. doi:10.1016/j.iheduc.2006.06.005. Retrieved from http://www.sciencedirect.com/science/article/pii/S1096751606000364

Son, J.-B., Robb, T., Hubbard, P., Stevens, V., & Seburn, T. (2015, March). Self-directed professional development in computer-assisted language learning. Colloquium conducted at the TESOL 2015 International Convention & English Language Expo, Metro Toronto Convention Centre, Toronto, Canada.

Steel, C., & Levy, M. (2013). Language students and their technologies: Charting the evolution 2006–2011. *ReCALL, 25*, 306–320. doi:10.1017/S0958344013000128

Teachers of English to Speakers of Other Languages, Inc. (TESOL). (2008). TESOL Technology Standards Framework. Retrieved from http://www.tesol.org/docs/books/bk_technologystandards_framework_721.pdf

Thomas, M., Reinders, H., & Warschauer, M. (Eds.) (2013). *Contemporary computer-assisted language learning*. London: Bloomsbury.

Thormann, J. (2009, December 11). Should you let students lead discussion boards? *Faculty Focus*. Retrieved from http://www.facultyfocus.com/articles/asynchronous-learning-and-trends/should-you-let-students-lead-discussion-boards/

Thormann, J. (2014, April 8). Encouraging online learner participation. *Faculty Focus*. Retrieved from http://www.facultyfocus.com/articles/asynchronous-learning-and-trends/encouraging-online-learner-participation/

Vygotsky, L. (1978). *Mind in society*. London: Harvard University Press.

Warschauer, M. (2002). A developmental perspective on technology in language education. *TESOL Quarterly 36*(3), 453–475.

10

An Invitation to CALL

Foundations of Computer-Assisted Language Learning

Philip Hubbard
Stanford University, USA

Introduction

In 1998, I began to offer a 'CALL mini-course' as a complement to Linguistics 191/291: Linguistics and the Teaching of English as a Second/Foreign Language, an ESL/EFL methodology class I had been teaching every winter since 1987 at Stanford University. The purpose was to bring in the growing influence of technology, not through the latest and greatest software or websites, but by drawing on an understanding of key concepts within the field. However, given the more tenuous position of technology in language teaching at that time, I made it an optional 1-unit seminar instead of a required part of the course.

Over the years, technology became more and more integrated into language teaching and learning, and I began to include more examples of computer-assisted language learning (CALL) into the core portion of the methodology class (see http://web.stanford.edu/~efs/ling291 for the most recent version of it). However, I felt that the bulk of the CALL portion needed to remain somewhat independent for two reasons. First, I have had other students as well as lecturers from my own ESL support programme in the class who were interested in CALL but neither wanted nor in some cases needed the content in the linguistics ESL/EFL course. Second, the university's quarter system with only ten weeks per term for classwork did not provide enough time to cover second language acquisition (SLA) methodology, and CALL at the level I wanted them. So CALL remained separated overall and voluntary. In a recent year, half of the credit students took the CALL course, along with four auditors, a fairly common combination. The course rarely exceeds ten participants and has had as few as two. This is one reason why I have made the full range of course material freely available worldwide on the web.

As a 'mini-course' it fills a space between the full CALL courses or course sequences noted in other chapters of this volume and the one-off technology unit sometimes found in a methodology course. The amount of time spent overall is not significant, but by bringing technology to the forefront and spreading the material across eight weeks, there is room for a participant to develop a clearer understanding of the place of that technology in their language teaching approach. It is not an online course (we meet face-to-face weekly) but the content is all online.

Context

This course has two audiences. The primary one in terms of design, though not numbers, consists of the students at Stanford University who take the CALL course directly as a complement to the Linguistics 191/291 ESL/EFL methodology class. This class typically has a mix of undergraduate and graduate students (hence the double number: Stanford uses 100-level numbers for upper-division undergraduate and 200-level for graduates). However, a second and hopefully much larger group are teacher educators who use the materials as a supplement to their own CALL and methodology classes, or teachers or developers who choose to approach the field on their own or collaboratively with colleagues. The course materials are all contained on a website, essentially a very thin introductory textbook with many annotated links to external sources (see later).

After teaching locally for five years, I released the information on this site publicly at a poster session at WorldCALL 2003 in Banff. A couple of iterations later, I set it up as a separate website that would serve both my students and the external audience. I gave it the name 'An invitation to CALL: Foundations of computer-assisted language learning'. Although I do not use 'Creative Commons', the terms of use are quite generous. I maintain copyright and ask that those using it acknowledge it as my work and do not sell it in printed form for more than the price of copying it (of course I have no way to enforce that). For anyone interested in its history, the oldest existing version, from early 2001, is available through the Internet archive at http://bit.ly/1HH2DyO (note that the course was renumbered from 289 to its present 191/291 in 2006).

I have presented the course several times at the annual TESOL Conference Internet Fairs, most recently in the 'Classics' sessions. I have been told by a number of both teacher trainers and independent teachers that they use it, though I do not keep a counter of hits. Some have even requested certificates of completion, something I am unable to provide as there is no mechanism for judging the degree to which the material was learned. Because my understanding of how others may be using it is limited, I focus most of this chapter on how it provides the core of my CALL mini-course at Stanford. I encourage interested readers to explore it on their own.

Course description

Although the structure shifted a bit during the first few years, it has long since settled into a regular eight-unit (usually eight-week) seminar with weekly meetings of sixty, seventy-five, or ninety minutes (seventy-five the most common) depending on student and instructor schedules. A major restructuring occurred in 2011 to catch up with the reality of essentially everything being online, and the URL for the course since then has been http://web.stanford.edu/~efs/callcourse2. The result is the current incarnation on that website, which is updated annually from January-March when the course is taught and irregularly throughout the rest of the year (usually for egregious errors someone has pointed out, but occasionally for exciting new information).

The introductory material prior to the first unit describes the course briefly along with its connection to the methodology class. As with following eight units of the core, the material is offered as a 'Web 1.0' html-based site but includes the option for viewing, copying or printing as a pdf. The introduction also includes recommendations for using the material independently as well as the terms of use for those outside the class.

Unit 1, An Introduction to Computer-Assisted Language Learning, is exactly that. It introduces Levy's (1997) tutor-tool framework as a starting point and then discusses a range of acronyms and attitudes in the field (CELL, TELL, TALL, CALI, CBLT, IT/ICT, NBLT, DLL, MALL – see http://web.stanford.edu/~efs/callcourse2/CALL1.htm for definitions) before settling on calling CALL 'CALL' throughout the rest of the course (Levy and Hubbard, 2005). This is followed by a brief sketch of CALL history from the 1960s onward to help participants understand some of the key shifts in technology and methodology that have shaped the field. Another section in this unit discusses the range of roles that teachers can have beyond that of consumers of others' work. Connected to that is an overview of the TESOL Technology Standards (TESOL, 2008), which are integrated throughout the course. The unit concludes with examples of recommended books, journals and other resources to give participants a sense of the range of research and practice materials. Unit 1, like the others, includes an assignment for participants to do before the next session. Besides reviewing the notes and links, to give them an initial experience with CALL, I ask them to try learning a bit of a *new* language through web-based or mobile app software (www.byki.com and www.duolingo.com are suggested). They spend at least an hour divided across two to three shorter sessions and come prepared the next class to discuss their experience.

In the second class meeting, we begin by reviewing the key points from Unit 1 and go over the homework with the language learning software, discussing individual and collective experiences. This is the class structure throughout the next few weeks – review and discussion followed by a skim through the new unit content, with most of the class time devoted to discussion, student presentation of their experiences and instructor demonstration with only limited amounts of lecture. Then we launch into Unit 2, the theme of which is finding and evaluating CALL resources. It opens by introducing Goal 2, Standard 1 of the TESOL Technology Standards (TESOL, 2008), which states: 'Language teachers identify and evaluate technological resources and environments for suitability to their teaching context.' The next part of the unit focuses on identifying resources, introducing a number of useful reference sites as well as checking with participants on their understanding of advanced search techniques using Google. In the following section on identifying environments, we cover the overall technology environment with specific reference to Stanford's local facilities, the online environment of the Internet and the mobile environment. Relevant to both the online and mobile environments, we discuss issues of security and ethics, touching on TESOL's Technology Standards for Teachers (Goal 1, Standard 4) regarding legal and ethical use of technology in language education. Participants are often surprised to discover that teacher use of many popular websites and apps for sharing student work violates US federal law regarding privacy of student data.

The second half of Unit 2 is devoted to evaluating courseware and other resources. This is an area I have been interested in since the late 1980s, and I introduce students to an evaluation framework I initially developed in that era that has been revised and updated several times since, with the most recent version in Hubbard (2011). This methodological framework is aimed at connecting the rich description of the material and its lesson flow, control and help options to concepts of learner fit and teacher fit. Rather than presenting a fixed checklist biased towards particular conceptions of those domains, it identifies areas to address to determine the degree of the consistency with the instructor's language teaching approach, syllabus and local learner characteristics. Although initially targeted at language courseware, it has since been expanded to web-based resources and to some degree technology-mediated language tasks (Hubbard, 2011). This unit includes a discussion of the value of appropriately designed checklists and an overview of an influential evaluation framework for CALL tasks and activities developed by Chapelle (2001). Rather than having a methodological base, her six-category framework reflects a set of principles derived from interactionist SLA theory and is used both for judgmental purposes and to evaluate learner outcomes. The unit also touches on a framework for evaluating websites by Son (2005), highlighting his concept of *authority*. Unit 2 concludes with a brief discussion of development and implementation considerations and a few additional resources for evaluation. The homework assignment is to critically read a published courseware or website review from the *CALICO Journal* or another professional source and determine the value of the information provided there in making a decision regarding whether to try it out in a particular setting. Essentially, it is a review of a review.

Computer-mediated communication (CMC) is a major branch of CALL. Unit 3 reviews this topic, linking to TESOL Standards for both language learners (Goal 3, Standard 3) and teachers (Goal 4, Standard 1). It opens with a discussion of text-based CMC, distinguishing asynchronous (e.g., email and discussion boards) from synchronous (chat). For asynchronous modes, it discusses options for peer to peer email exchanges for classes such as www.epals.com and www.interpals.net. It also notes a range of options for asynchronous discussion including not only dedicated discussion boards such as those found in learning management systems like Moodle but also posting to media sites, blogs and social networks. For synchronous chat, it cites early work showing that interaction in such environments is more evenly distributed in locally networked than in face-to-face settings and that text-based chat can support a wider range of discourse functions than face-to-face oral interaction in the same kind of task (Kern, 1995).

The next section covers audio and video CMC, using the same asynchronous versus synchronous distinction. Although there are sites like www.voicethread.com and www.voxopop.com that support asynchronous CMC through audio and video, the use of free synchronous connections like Apple's FaceTime,

Microsoft's Skype and Google's Hangouts seems to be growing rapidly for language education. This is especially the case with online and blended environments, where the technical quality of video interaction between teachers and students or among peer learners has improved markedly over the past few years. As is pointed out in the final section on integrating CMC into classes, research has unveiled some interesting characteristics of text-based interaction in particular. So-called synchronous chat is not really synchronous: the typed message is generally not sent until the user hits the enter key, allowing time for reflection and 'self-initiated self-repair' (Smith, 2008, p. 85) not possible in either face-to-face or arguably in synchronous audio or video modes. In addition, it has been noted that some tasks are clearly better than others for generating negotiation of meaning, that students are likely to use technologies in ways they are already familiar with rather than in ways intended by teachers, and that cross-class (especially cross-cultural) online interactions can fail as well as succeed depending on various factors such as differences in language level and accessibility. The homework for this unit is to visit one of several online chat rooms or discussion boards targeted at language learners, reviewing the interactions there for language learning potential and participating in at least one such interaction.

Unit 4 covers CALL and language skills. It begins by asking students to address three questions relevant to this topic:

1) What have teachers/developers done to teach the skill areas using computers?
2) To what extent does what they've done actually enhance learning?
3) And most important, how can you use these resources to support your students' learning objectives?

This is followed by a discussion of ESL portals, collections of links to online English materials categorized across multiple skill levels, such as www.manythings.org and www.eslgold.com. The four core skills of listening, speaking, reading and writing along with grammar, pronunciation, vocabulary and culture are then each briefly described along with representative examples of tasks and resources as summarized below.

- Listening. This is potentially one of the most promising areas for CALL development. Although commercial multimedia materials and teacher-produced sites such as www.esl-lab.com and www.elllo.org remain popular, much interested has shifted from these to authentic materials found on sites like YouTube and www.ted.com. Help options such as transcripts, captions and the ability to manipulate speed with a media player have aided work on comprehension and associated vocabulary building.

- Speaking. As noted in the CMC unit, speaking practice is supported by audio discussion boards and synchronous voice and video through Skype and similar applications. Tandem learning sites like www.mylanguageexchange.com allow learners to connect with others learning their language for a collaborative experience. Indirectly, speaking is supported through the wide range of video materials on YouTube and elsewhere that provide models for situated communicative interaction.
- Reading. At one time reading digitally was considered a poor substitute for paper text, but increasingly reading on everything from laptops to tablets to smartphones is commonplace. Digital reading offers language learners the potential for instant access to word meanings through pop-up dictionaries. Skill-building applications for text reconstruction such as cloze and jigsaw exercises as well as timed and paced reading are available. Sites such as www.er-central.com provide English language learners with free graded readers and support materials.
- Writing. Arguably word processing was the first technology application to become ubiquitous in language learning classes. Now second language writing development is supported by text-based CMC tasks, collaborative environments like wikis and Google docs and opportunities to write for authentic audiences through blogs and social media tools.
- Grammar. In the early days of CALL, grammar drill and practice was a mainstay of the field. Workbook-style exercises, grammar test-prep materials and CD-ROMs and online support for grammar textbooks remain.
- Pronunciation. Technology makes a number of help and feedback options available targeted at improving pronunciation. There are digital versions of 'listen-repeat/record-replay' for comparison with a model. Visualization of the speech signal as a wave form, spectrogram (voice print) or pitch contour add a graphic dimension to sound that can be helpful. Speech recognition systems such as those at www.englishcentral.com can provide useful feedback on pronunciation accuracy in the absence of a teacher or tutor.
- Vocabulary. Due to the discrete nature of lexical items, vocabulary development is among the best supported areas of CALL. Electronic dictionaries (both L1 and L2) and various applications for selecting and reviewing vocabulary are available. Google images can provide support beyond the text mode. Mobile apps make it possible to learn and review vocabulary in small chunks of free time during the day.

- Culture. The web is awash with authentic cultural material even for less commonly taught languages. Sights and sounds of the environments where the target language is spoken are readily available through YouTube and other sources. The MIT Cultura Project (http://cultura.mit.edu) has been operating since 1997 to connect classes for cultural exchanges.

The homework assignment for this unit is to select one skill area, review the links on the course website and then go online to find one or two additional ones that are relevant to share with the class.

Unit 5 covers the topics of CALL environments, tools, materials and activities. In versions prior to 2011, this was Unit 4 'CALL on the Web' (see http://web.stanford.edu/~efs/callcourse/CALL4.htm). It was clear by 2010 that *most* of CALL was on the web in one way or another, so the title and much of the content were changed accordingly. The first section on environments references TESOL's Goal 2, Standard 1 mentioned for Unit 2, as well as Goal 1, Standard 2 referring to teachers' knowledge of 'a wide range' of technology options and especially their ability to use those options 'in a given setting'. Environments touched on include classrooms, computer centers, dedicated language labs, student homes, cafes and other wireless connectivity spots and mobile computing. In the section on tools, only a few are touched on, such as dictionaries, machine translation and concordance and other lexical tools found on Tom Cobb's enormously useful Compleat Lexical Tutor site: www.lextutor.ca. Materials are divided between authentic language materials found everywhere on the web (e.g., news and entertainment, YouTube, podcasts) and dedicated language materials and exercises including tutorial software, some of which were noted in Unit 4. The materials section also includes a segment on collecting, tagging and especially curating digital content. Finally, the section on activities provides advice and resources to explore for projects, lesson plans and website creation, along with links to websites of CALL experts. For homework, participants search through provided links or on Google for sample activities or lesson plans they could use in a relevant setting.

Having established a rich basis in CALL practice, in Unit 6 we shift to CALL theory and research. It begins by referencing a key TESOL Technology Standard: 'Language teachers use relevant research findings to inform the planning of language learning tasks and activities that involve technology' (Goal 2, Standard 4). I then introduce a conception of theory from Hubbard (2009) as follows:

> Collectively, *CALL theory* is the set of perspectives, models, frameworks, and specific theories that offer generalizations to account for phenomena related to

> the use of computers and the pursuit of language learning objectives, to ground relevant research agendas, and to inform effective CALL design and practice ... [whereas] *a* CALL theory is a set of claims about the meaningful elements and processes within some domain of CALL, their interrelationships, and the impact that they have on language learning development and outcomes. (p. 3)

Participants learn that there is no established 'CALL theory' similar to those in SLA or linguistics. Instead, I explain that most of the theoretical basis of CALL comes from borrowing theories from cognate disciplines, especially cognitivist, constructivist or sociocultural theories from SLA. The unit continues with a typology incorporating a fuller range of theoretical sources for research, development and practice.

The section on research begins by noting that while some research is merely exploratory, studying existing student and teacher attitudes and uses of technology for language learning are, most is interventional, testing a task, activity, software application and so on to see whether it leads to 'better' language learning. I define 'better' for them as meeting one or more of the following criteria.

- Learners pick up language knowledge or skills faster or with less effort (learning efficiency)
- Learners pick up what is targeted, retain language knowledge or skills longer, and/or learn more of what they need (effectiveness)
- Learners can get materials or experience interactions that would otherwise be difficult or impossible (access)
- Learners can learn with more or less equal effectiveness across a wider range of times/places (convenience)
- Learners enjoy the language learning process more or are willing to engage in it more (motivation)
- Learners require less space, less teacher time or less expensive materials (institutional efficiency)

This list provides a sort of rough evaluation metric for sorting through the technical details of published research.

The unit continues with a list of several research trends and then offers two tables containing example studies, a description of the content of each, and some of the key results. The first table includes studies from the early 2000s and the second, ones from 2008–2011. The remaining four brief sections cover a survey of unanswered questions in CALL I conducted in 2002 (http://web.stanford.edu/~efs/callsurvey/), a review of subject characteristics in CALL research, advice on doing research and suggestions for locating desired research studies. The assignment is to go to the survey of unanswered questions site, review at least three of the sixty-four questions there, and then pick one, searching Google Scholar to see what answers, if any, may have been provided for it in the years since.

Unit 7 on the old course site was devoted to the topic of learner training, but in its present incarnation, teacher education and professional development have been added as well. Participants are reminded of the range of roles they can have with respect to CALL, including becoming CALL specialists or professionals. The concept of 'technological pedagogical content knowledge' for CALL is introduced (see http://www.tpack.org/) along with additional options for teacher education and further discussion of standards. The 2015 special issue of *Language Learning & Technology* on CALL teacher education is highlighted (http://llt.msu.edu/issues/february2015/index.html).

Professional development in CALL rather than teacher education per se is likely to be more relevant for many of the participants (four of six in a recent class were already practicing teachers). Not surprisingly, the TESOL Technology Standards promote this explicitly. Teacher Goal 4, Standard 2 states: 'Language teachers regularly reflect on the intersection of professional practice and technological developments so that they can make informed decisions regarding the use of technology to support language learning and communication.' Goal 1, Standard 3 says: 'Language teachers actively strive to expand their skill and knowledge base to evaluate, adopt, and adapt emerging technologies throughout their careers.' The section on this topic reviews a range of options for accomplishing those goals. These include online resources, communities of practice, professional organizations, workshops and classes, readings, and my personal favourite, individual and collaborative projects.

The final section shifts from teacher to learner training. On a personal note, this is an area that has intrigued me for quite some time, but it remains surprisingly ignored by much of the CALL literature. After making a case for why learner training is desirable and explaining why technical training alone is insufficient, I introduce students to a framework I developed (Hubbard, 2004) based on five principles: experience CALL yourself, give learners teacher training, use a cyclical approach, use collaborative debriefings, and teach general exploitation strategies. I conclude with an update on that framework that divides learner training into three domains instead of two: technical, strategic and pedagogical.

Besides covering key parts of the content for Unit 7 on the website, we spend some time discussing the course project during this class (see below for more details). Students taking the course for credit and doing projects have already had their topics approved by me in advance of this and come to the class prepared to give a preliminary report. Time is set aside for them to describe their project and progress briefly, and peers provide encouragement and feedback. With three or fewer presenters, this is a whole class activity; otherwise, students divide into groups for the discussion.

The final class (Unit 8) features the project presentations, which typically take up about half the class time. Rather than conducting the typical review with the remaining time, I use it instead to cover areas of the field missed in the previous seven units. Concordancing, or data-driven learning, is an area of particular interest to the linguistics majors in the course, and I introduce them to http://www.lextutor.ca/conc/eng/ as an example of an online concordancer. Participants are already familiar with the learning management system (LMS) they use at Stanford, but since some will be teaching overseas, I mention Moodle as an example of an LMS widely used to support language teaching. Computer-based language assessment is also touched on, in line with TESOL's Goal 3, Standard 1 regarding teacher familiarity with technology-based assessment options. Two other themes addressed in this part are the value of student tracking and using technology to help develop learner autonomy. The course concludes with a look at four rapidly emerging areas, some of which were touched on in earlier units: social networks, mobile learning, virtual worlds and gaming. It emphasizes the fact that we cannot really predict where the field is going in the next few years and how important it is to prepare for a future of constant change and lifelong learning as a technology-using teacher.

Features and issues

The previous section has provided most of the pertinent details of the course and all the information is available on the aforementioned course website. However, there are a few special features of this course worth noting. These involve its focus on foundational concepts rather than just current technology, its ability both to stand alone and to integrate into a methodology course, the links to the TESOL Technology Standards, the goal of covering the field in a broad but shallow manner, and the requirement of an individual project for those taking the course for credit.

CALL like every field has a history. However, because it is so tightly connected with whatever the current technology is, the subject is often taught without sufficient attention to that history. Not only in the first unit, but throughout the course there are references to relevant material from past decades. This runs against a common trend in both courses and textbooks, which seem to focus much more heavily on the current state of the field. By viewing the development of the field through the personal lens of having worked in it since the early 1980s and sharing that with the class, I hope to provide a grounding that will deflect the otherwise natural tendency to jump onto the most recent technological bandwagon assuming that it will revolutionize language learning all by itself.

Not only are the TESOL Technology Standards integrated into this course, they were in some minor ways influenced by it (see TESOL, 2008) for details of how the Standards were developed. As one of the six members of the Standards writing team, I relied heavily on my own CALL teaching experience to help articulate the Standards and accompanying performance indicators. I began formally integrating them into the mini-course several years after TESOL published them and found it interesting to see where the course hit and in some cases missed the Standards. I have made some minor adjustments in the past three years to bring the two closer, though there are still some gaps (not surprising in a course with only eight to twelve contact hours). Beginning in 2014, I have had participants fill out the set of 'can do' statements in the latest Standards book (Healey et al., 2011). In the follow-up discussions, I was able to see some variation in what they were and were not confident about, but almost universally there was little knowledge of the CALL research base or engagement with communities of practice. It also became clear that several of the expectations of the Standards were unrealistic for teachers in training who were not actively in a classroom.

With respect to the scope of the course, at the time I began teaching it in 1998, a number of other CALL courses reported on at conferences and in publications were focusing primarily on how to develop websites and accompanying tasks or run CMC sessions. An example of this 'depth-first' approach can be found in Chao (2006), who describes a CALL course exclusively devoted to the topic of developing WebQuests. As someone who had begun his CALL career as a courseware developer and was still authoring CD-ROMs in the late 1990s, I wanted to be sure to cover the tutorial side of CALL while accommodating the increasing use of computers as mediating tools, and to do so across all skills. I also wanted teachers to have at least an idea of the types of research available to them to inform CALL practice. For that reason, I opted for a 'breadth-first' survey of the field approach of the type found in introductory academic courses like psychology or linguistics. Students who want greater depth in a particular area can do so by pursuing the many links to external resources on their own or more ideally through the course project.

The project has been mentioned previously, but I would like to provide some more detail here. It is required for course credit and optional for non-credit participants. I introduce it briefly at the beginning, but it becomes a more central feature around Week 5 when participants have a solid base on which to start building it. Students are offered a menu of pre-approved topics but may also negotiate something different if they wish. The pre-approved ones are the following:

1) Critically reviewing a CALL book or a major article
2) Evaluating a piece of software (CD-ROM, mobile app or web application) or website for language learning using the framework in Unit 2
3) Designing and justifying a language learning application, website or technology-based task
4) Designing and actually programming an application or building a website

In addition to presenting at the last class, students need to provide a write-up of the project. Topics (1) and (2) require a longer paper than do (3) and (4).

Turning now to issues, the most significant one is that this is a very personal course from my side (as the reference list will attest). I warn both students and outside users up front in the introductory material that CALL is too young and dynamic to have a reliable 'core curriculum' for such a limited course as ours. I have been active in the field for a number of years and the material on the course website mirrors to some extent my personal experiences. I have written elsewhere (Hubbard, 2008) about the range of approaches teacher educators can take to bringing students into the field, and, as noted above, I selected the breadth first, survey style one. Because of this, and the fact that there are no exams or projects that sample comprehensive understanding, I am concerned that participants may soon forget elements that they did not engage with as fully as others. The only support I can offer for that eventuality is to leave the course material up for those who wish to return later.

Finally, there are clearly some parts that are much thinner than others in their coverage. Given its importance in the field, the CMC unit deserves to be enriched and updated more. Similarly, the unit on language skills is more superficial than I would like, and the section on tools in Unit 5 was recently added and needs some major expansion. The set of technologies noted in Unit 8 are really just explained, and as it is the last class, students are left to their own devices to follow up on those.

Future directions

Every year I revise and update the course as I teach it, and this is my intention for as long as I end up continuing with it. It is a bit behind the times in some areas, notably in its limited coverage of MALL and game-based learning, and I plan to expand those. I would also like to find ways to address all of the TESOL Technology Standards. The biggest limitation for me is how to keep true to the course's claim of breadth while still staying within the eight-unit, 8–12 contact hour range needed by the academic structure it is embedded in. One option would be to start building the course more hierarchically, with links to optional modules in areas that are currently underserved.

Because of having so few students of my own, I have made the course materials as freely available as possible and will continue to do so. If time allows, future versions might have enriched activities to support the explanatory text and bring it more to life. The title of the website remains An invitation to CALL: Foundations of computer-assisted language learning, and I hope that it is consistent with that implied promise. For those who know little about the field, it provides a relatively quick way for them to become familiar with a wide range of options that technology avails us, along with some suggested resources and activities to trigger reflection on both the strengths and weaknesses of a given application of technology in their particular environments. Even for those who know a lot, it may help to fill some gaps.

The site for the linguistics version of the CALL mini course described here is http://web.stanford.edu/~efs/ling291/call.html. From there course participants link to the public Invitation to CALL site at http://web.stanford.edu/~efs/callcourse2/. I encourage interested readers to explore them.

References

Chapelle, C. (2001). *Computer applications in second language acquisition.* Cambridge: Cambridge University Press.

Chao, C.-C. (2006). How WebQuests send technology to the background: Scaffolding EFL teacher professional development in CALL. In P. Hubbard & M. Levy (Eds.), *Teacher education in CALL* (pp. 221–234). Amsterdam: John Benjamins.

Healey, D., Hanson-Smith, E., Hubbard, P., Ioannou-Georgiou, S., Kessler, G., & Ware, P. (2011). *TESOL Technology standards: Description, implementation, integration.* Alexandria, VA: TESOL.

Hubbard, P. (2004). Learner training for effective use of CALL. In S. Fotos & C. Browne (Eds.), *New perspectives on CALL for second language classrooms* (pp. 45–68). Mahwah, NJ: Lawrence Erlbaum.

Hubbard, P. (2008). CALL and the future of language teacher education. *CALICO Journal, 25*(2), 175–188.

Hubbard, P. (2009). Developing CALL theory: A new frontier. *Proceedings of the JALTCALL Conference.* Tokyo: JALTCALL.

Hubbard, P. (2011). Evaluation of courseware and websites. In N. Arnold & L. Ducate (Eds.), *Present and future promises of CALL: From theory and research to new directions in language teaching* (pp. 407–440). San Marcos, TX: CALICO.

Kern, R. G. (1995). Restructuring classroom interaction with networked computers: Effects on quantity and characteristics of language production. *The Modern Language Journal, 79*(4), 457–476.

Levy, M. (1997). *Computer-assisted language learning: Context and conceptualization.* New York: Oxford University Press.

Levy, M., & Hubbard, P. (2005). Why call CALL 'CALL'? *Computer Assisted Language Learning, 18*(3), 143–149.

Smith, B. (2008). Methodological hurdles in capturing CMC data: The case of the missing self-repair. *Language Learning & Technology, 12*(1), 85–103.

Son, J.-B. (2005). Exploring and evaluating language learning websites. In J.-B. Son & S. O'Neill (Eds.), *Enhancing learning and teaching: Pedagogy, technology and language* (pp. 215–227). Flaxton, Australia: Post Pressed. Retrieved from http://www.apacall.org/member/sonjb/papers/Son_ch13_2005.pdf.

TESOL (2008). *TESOL technology standards framework.* Alexandria, VA: TESOL. Retrieved from https://www.tesol.org/docs/books/bk_technologystandards_framework_721.pdf

11

Should We Offer a CALL Course?

Denise E. Murray
Macquarie University, Australia

Introduction

While the Digital Divide has narrowed over the past decade with 42.4 per cent of the world's population having Internet access as of December 2014 (Internet World Stats, 2015) compared with 18.9 per cent in 2007, physical access, bandwidth and digital device vary across countries and within countries. A recent study in California (Avalos, 2015) found that 21 per cent had no broadband access and 8 per cent had access only via smartphones, which do not allow for 'productivity tasks, or kids doing school work' (p. B6). They found that those with less education, low income levels and disabilities are the most likely to have inadequate access to broadband. Therefore, we can 'never assume that all students have access to all new technologies' (Kim, Rueckert, Kim, & Seo, 2013, p. 60). Despite this caveat, the growth in the use of computer-assisted language learning (CALL) is evidenced by the number of CALL-specific journals, recent volumes and standards for the use of technology in language teaching (Healey et al., 2011). Therefore, it is likely that teachers and other educators are likely to need to understand the role of CALL. This need has already been acknowledged not only in this volume and the edited volume of Hubbard and Levy (2006b), but also in methodology texts (see, for example, Tomlinson, 2011) and volumes on general second language teacher education (see, for example, Burns & Richards, 2009). In fact, one of the most persistent findings in research in CALL has been the need for ongoing professional development for teachers (see, for example, Healey et al., 2011; Peters, 2006). But, what do language teachers need to know about and be able to do with CALL? Emerging from this question is how language teachers acquire this knowledge and skills.

The role of teacher education

There is an extensive literature on the impact of both pre- and in-service teacher professional development. The consensus is that professional development opportunities need to be sustained, continuous and coherent (see, for example, Edge, 2002). Further, the consensus is that to be effective, such professional development needs to address both content and process (see, e.g., Richards & Nunan, 1990) so that teachers know how to make informed decisions in new and unpredictable situations. In other words, professional development is a life-long learning enterprise. To make such informed choices in CALL, language teachers need more than 'how to' manuals or lists of computer applications or CALL software or websites with instructional materials. Hubbard (Chapter 10, this volume) seems to concur when he says that he chose to introduce teachers to CALL 'not through the latest and greatest software or websites, but by drawing on an understanding of key concepts within the field'.

Teachers need to identify, explore, discuss and critically evaluate the issues in CALL. They need to examine these issues in relation to their own teaching context and those of their peers. These contexts may vary from low resourced, to mobile only, to elaborated Learning Management Systems (LMS), to bring your own device (BYOD), to institution-provided tablets for each student, to hard-wired computer labs, to one hard-wired computer in a classroom. Finally, CALL teachers need to reflect on their own practice and use of CALL. Any CALL-specific course needs to situate CALL in both language pedagogy and the protean nature of technologies. In other words, the goal of CALL teacher education must be the development of a critical understanding of the affordances and limitations of CALL. Such coursework needs to go beyond the acquisition of skills; rather it needs to involve the application of principles to different CALL activities. If CALL is becoming mainstream, rather than 'a niche field practised by a few early adopters' (Motteram, 2013b, p. 6), then CALL needs to be integrated across the teacher education curriculum. However, as Hubbard and Levy (2006b) pointed out, institutional constraints usually mean CALL courses in language teacher education tend to be stand alone, as illustrated by the courses documented in this volume.

As can be seen in the chapters in this volume, CALL teacher education has been approached from a number of different theoretical perspectives, such as SLA (see Chapter 6, this volume) or social constructivism (see Chapters 7 and 8, this volume). Motteram, Slaouti and Onat-Stelmal (2013) also argue for a sociocultural perspective in CALL teacher education on the grounds that second language teacher education is increasingly using sociocultural theory in its practice. Pegrum (2014), on the other hand, recommends the Technological Pedagogical Content Knowledge (TPCK) framework of knowledge integration and the Substitution Augmentation Modification Redefinition (SAMR) model of technological transformation (Puentedura, 2011). The SAMR model examines technology in terms of its effects on language pedagogy, whether it enhances or transforms such pedagogy.

The content and process of CALL teacher education are discussed below. However, an overarching issue must first be addressed: the changing context for CALL and for CALL teacher education.

The constancy of change

One of the challenges in both using CALL and teaching about CALL is its ever changing nature, as the authors in this volume recognize. As teacher educators, we are left with a dilemma: the technology is changing so rapidly that if we build a course around applications, we may well find that those applications have become obsolete or at least superseded by the time our students begin their teaching. On the other hand, student teachers look to us for guidance on what technology to use, when and how (Colpaert, 2014). Several of the chapters in this volume document decades-long course development. These curricula changes show how not only the technology has changed, but also how our understandings of language learning and teaching have changed. In their examination of historical perspectives on CALL, Davies, Otto and Rüssoff (2013) note that '[w]hile the evolution of computer technology can be described in a relatively linear and organized fashion, SLA and language pedagogy have developed as a disorganized, multipronged and often contradictory collection of notions and practices' (p. 19). Additionally, the students in our CALL teacher education classes have changed, as noted in many of the chapters in this volume. Today, '[d]igital natives respond well to technology-infused activities because of their familiarity with technology' (Prensky, 2001). While many are 'digital natives', many have limited knowledge of and practical experiences with all computer-based technology. As Kim et al. (2013) have cautioned about assuming all language students have access to all new technologies, this is equally true for students in teacher education.

For both language learners and students in teacher education classes, access is broader than physical access. The term Digital Divide has been 'repurposed to refer to the gap between those with the skills to make effective use of digital technologies, and those who lack such skills' (Hockly, Dudeney, & Pegrum, 2013, p. 15).

Despite the disorganisation that Davies et al. identify, several language educators have tried to capture the interplay between technology, language pedagogy and SLA. Warschauer (1996), for example, proposed three stages of CALL with their dominant technology, underlying English language teaching pedagogy and theories of language. The three stages he designated as behaviourist (1970s–1980s), communicative (1980s–1990s), and integrative (21st century). For the 21st century, he identified the dominant technology as multimedia and the Internet. However, because this proposal was first suggested in 1996 and updated in 2001, he was not able to predict the explosion of social media. At issue in such a depiction is whether the stages are a result of the technology available at the time or because of the prevailing theories of language pedagogy and language. For example, for the stage he designated behaviourist, Warschauer identified the technology as mainframe, the pedagogy as grammar-translation and audiolingual and the theory of language as structural. As Davies et al. noted, language pedagogy does not neatly conform to periods. Grammar-translation has continued in actual classrooms and still exists. Similarly, while the majority of CALL implementation on mainframe computers was drill and practice, today drill and practice can be found on many websites that teach languages. Further, several innovations were in practice in the 1970s and 1980s, such as Higgins's (1984) Storyboard, published in 1982, which is neither drill and practice nor communicative. Considering the development of CALL over time through stages implies the teleology of the technology, an approach to technology that is deterministic, that the technology inevitably leads to changes in human thinking and behaviour. However, as Murray (2005, 2013) has noted, users of any technology appropriate the technology for their own purposes.

Because of these complexities, Warschauer's depiction of stages has been challenged by others, such as Motteram (2013b) and Bax (2003). Motteram argues that examining historical stages is less useful than viewing educational technologies as sociocultural activities that mediate classroom practice, while Bax provides an alternative to stages, namely, three approaches. These approaches are restricted CALL, open CALL and integrated CALL. Bax saw the early 2000s as being open CALL, but that the aim should be normalization, where the technology is invisible and completely integrated into teaching practice. In a more recent article, Bax (2011) questions the assumption that normalisation will necessarily result in better language learning outcomes. Instead, he proposes considering technology in language education from a neo-Vygotskian perspective, with older children and adults using technology to scaffold their learning of languages. In this same article, he later proposes elements of effective teaching practice that should be employed in the use of technology in language education. These elements can be used to determine whether a particular technology should be adopted or not:

- Access to and interaction with sources of prior knowledge or information is frequently important in learning;
- Participation and interaction with others, which includes a social and even an emotional dimension, is also frequently of value in education;
- Expert scaffolding: interaction with an expert, who actively 'scaffolds' the experience, through planning, feedback and advice, constantly checking that learning is taking place;
- Expert modelling: the example of an expert, who exemplifies in his/her own behaviour;
    - A set of approaches to knowledge and learning, including a criticality and rigour in dealing with sources of knowledge; and
    - A methodical and cautious mode of expression in communicating ideas and information to others, and who models this behaviour to the learner.
- Challenge and contradiction from an expert, and from other learners, in a way to cause the learner to rethink and review a position or idea (Bax, 2011).

Murray (2005) claimed that, although technologies are 'shaped by socio-economic, political, and cultural human agency' (p. 29), several emerging developments would likely be adopted in education:

- Broadband, because it would provide 'realia "just-in-time"' (p. 30).
- Convergence, where content and delivery mechanisms are controlled by the same corporations, with attendant issues of power and control.
- Wireless communication, along with improved battery storage, which leads to flexibility and mobility for teachers and learners.
- Miniaturization, which could lead to 'a more distributed systems peer-to-peer network typology' (p. 32).

These four developments have led to the widespread use of cell phones and tablets for education. However, while she predicted that these developments would lead to greater integration of technology in the language classrooms, she, too, like Warschauer, did not predict the explosion of social media. In hindsight, we can wonder why we did not imagine how people would co-opt the technology for communication and social interaction. If we examine the use of computer technology historically, we see the way people took a machine designed to make rapid calculations and turned it into a communications device. Email was a development from one-line messages sent by workers at dumb terminals, asking operators in the computer room to load a specific tape of data, for example. Very quickly workers began sending messages to each other if they were logged on at the same time. Once store and forward technology was developed, email developed. Similarly, the Internet, begun to allow for easier sharing of research data for the military, became a vehicle for communicating beyond workers in the same building.

More recently, Dudeney and Hockly (2012) have proposed the technological innovations that will have an impact on language education, namely mobile and blended learning; and augmented reality and game-based learning. However, these are currently available tools. Further, as we have seen with past innovations, we cannot predict how people will appropriate new technology for new and creative purposes.

Against this background of changing technology and complex interactions among theories of language, language learning and language learning pedagogy, what should be the content and processes in a CALL teacher education course or courses? The chapters in this volume provide a variety of different theoretical and practical perspectives on how to design such a course because, as Hubbard in Chapter 10 says, 'CALL is too young and dynamic to have a reliable core curriculum'. In the next sections, I propose content and processes, based on the earlier discussion.

CALL teacher education content

In 2006 Hubbard and Levy (2006a) stated that CALL teachers need both technical and pedagogical knowledge and skill. However, their definition of the technical knowledge was limited to understanding computer software, hardware and networking, while the pedagogical knowledge was 'understanding of ways of effectively using the computer in language teaching' (p. 16). I argue that, because of the complex interplay of computers, language and language learning, we need to include an understanding of this complexity. While not exhaustive, key issues that CALL teachers need to know include the changing nature of technology, including the contexts and history of CALL; the ability to evaluate materials; multiliteracies; and the affordances and limitations of CALL.

Changing nature of technology

For future CALL teachers to understand and use CALL in their own contexts, they need to learn about and discuss different contexts over time and across different social, economic and geographic settings. Language teachers work in many contexts, are often peripatetic and often include interaction with language learners in different contexts to help their learners access authentic language.

As discussed earlier, several approaches to CALL's development have been posited.

The changing nature of technology has been identified as an important issue to include in any CALL teacher education course in several chapters in this volume (e.g., Chapters 2, 5, 7). Even though some courses do not include this as a specific issue, the authors recognize it when they discuss their changing course structures and content over time (e.g., Chapter 9). As well as the changing nature of technology to, for example, mobile devices, language teachers need to understand how CALL has adapted over time, to both changes in language pedagogy and in technology. This need for teachers to have knowledge of CALL history is reflected in many of the chapters in this volume (e.g., Chapters 2, 3, 4, 6, 9, 10).

Materials evaluation

One of the most frequently cited task evaluation criteria are those of Chappelle (2001):

- language learning potential, the degree of opportunity present for beneficial focus on form
- learner fit, the amount of opportunity for engagement with language under appropriate conditions given learn characteristics
- meaning focus, the extent to which learners' attention is directed towards meaning
- authenticity, the degree of correspondence between learning activity and target language activities of interest to students outside the classroom
- positive impact, the positive effects of CALL activity on those engaged in it, and
- practicality, the adequacy of resources to support use of the CALL activity.

More recently, but in a similar vein, Hockly (2013) discusses six essential parameters for the design of communicative tasks using mobile devices: hardware, mobility, technological complexity, linguistic complexity, type of mobile-assisted language learning and education context (p. 9).

In addition to evaluating materials, there are many different models for evaluating websites. In fact, most universities provide some sort of guidelines. Most of them consider accuracy, authority, objectivity and currency, rather than actual design (see, for example, Cornell University Library, 2015). Webpage design and readability has been studied largely by researchers providing criteria for Webpage designers for commerce such as the lab of Jacob Nielsen (Nielsen, 2003), that has been studying design for more than a decade.

Multiliteracies

Motteram (2013a) says, 'In order to access the web effectively, to gain maximum language learning from any material or activity, we need to make sure that the learners have the necessary skills to be able to approach and interpret a text' (p. 186). While Motteram did not expand on his definition of 'text', I argue that text includes the multimodal literacy needed to engage in computer-mediated communication (CMC), to navigate the web to read, and read the web to navigate (see Lipscomb, 2005, for a research study in which she developed this notion). We are in the early stages of understanding the influence of multimodality on our lives, on learning and on making meaning from such texts. However, we do know that such skills go beyond what has traditionally been called digital literacy, such as defined in Chapter 9 this volume: ability to use computers (including mobile devices). The term multimodal literacy has been used, defined by Anstey and Bull (2011) as referring to any text that includes more than one semiotic system. While their definition is broader than digital literacies, it is also too broad for CALL since it includes texts such as a printed picture book. Research on online reading has shown it to be significantly different from print reading (see Tindale, 2005 for a summary of this research). CALL teachers therefore need to understand these differences and ways in which they can help their language learners acquire multimodal literacy in a new language, which the courses discussed in Chapters 3 and 9 in this volume recognize.

Affordances and limitations of CALL

In an article on autonomy, Reinders and White (2011) summarized the affordances of CALL, dividing them into two categories: organizational advantages and pedagogical advantages. While each of these aspects of CALL can facilitate or amplify language teaching and learning, each also brings with it possible limitations, of which prospective teachers need to be aware. Their organizational advantages are access, storage and retrieval of learning behaviour records and outcomes, sharing and recycling of materials and cost efficiency. The pedagogical advantages are authenticity, interaction, situated learning, multimedia, new types of activities, non-linearity, feedback, monitoring and recording of learning behaviour and progress, control and empowerment. Rather than discussing each affordance and its potential limitation, here I address only four of them as examples of the affordances and limitations teachers need to understand: access, authenticity, interaction and feedback.

New technologies allow learners (and teachers) to access more and richer resources than in print text. Traditionally, educators have been concerned about the digital divide (see, for example, Murray, 1999; Warschauer, 2000), the differential access to computer technology between rich and poor, old and young, urban and rural, educated and less educated, disabled and abled and dominant and minority groups that occurs both within and across nations. The advent of mobile devices has helped reduce that divide so that in 2014, 42.3 per cent of the world's population was online, compared with only 6 per cent in 1997 (Internet World Stats, 2015). However, despite this great promise, educators and others worry about two issues as discussed earlier: the gap in broadband access and the skills needed to effectively use digital technologies.

Authenticity refers to both interactions and materials, where learners are engaged with materials and people that are not artefacts of instruction. Warschauer's (2000) characterizes the principle uses of computers for CALL in the 21st integrated century as authentic discourse, but often that authentic discourse is language and behaviours that we do not want our learners exposed to, such as flaming. Examples of authentic interactions include learners collaborating on a project via discussion lists, Googledocs or email. Although the task may be an artefact of instruction, the interactions of collaboration are authentic communication. Educators have found that CMC in particular provides opportunities for authentic communication across geographical regions, promotes collaboration because it is asynchronous and is especially suitable for project-based learning (Debski, 2006). In addition to language learners interacting with their peers, they can interact with native speakers of the language they are learning, such as with keypals or by interviewing an expert. However, others have noted that collaboration needs to be carefully planned, scaffolded and should provide opportunities for learner reflection on the process (Schwienhorst, 2004), while others have noted that some learners are frustrated by having to work in groups (Felix, 2001). Technology provides learners with a vast array of materials in the target language, and authentic in that they were not designed for learning purposes. However, it is the very enormity of these materials that can be negative experiences for learners because of the level of language and content, and the difficulty of searching for materials that are reliable and from an authority.

Feedback is an essential component of learning. Technologies have made providing timely, multimodal, specific and personalized feedback easier. CALL programmes that act as tutors can provide such feedback in addition to the teacher. The recent development of ICALL using parsers has made it possible for such programmes to 'learn' about learners' progress and make feedback accordingly (Heift & Schulze, 2007). However, while these are possibilities, a large number of CALL tutoring programmes or exercise sites do little more than telling the learner yes or no.

In addition to the various issues in adopting CALL that teachers need to know, they also need technical knowledge and skills, as Hubbard and Levy identified (2006b). However, as discussed earlier, the rapidly changing technology, and the number and variety of its applications, presents a challenge. Many of the chapters in this volume relate many of these applications. While some have chosen to teach a wide range, others have chosen to primarily use technology to deliver their courses, such as an LMS. The latter has the advantage of being an authentic learning experience for the prospective teachers. However, as Murray and Christison (2017) found in their large-scale study of online language teacher education (OLTE), teacher educators and their students often find the LMS available at their institution to be inadequate for their preferred teaching and learning styles. Teacher educators, for example, ranked flexibility, transparency, messaging system and tools for synchronous tools as important features of an LMS, while the students placed a high priority on features that assist them in doing well in the courses, such as tracking progress and grades. While teacher educators wanted collaborative, interactive, group work, students wanted to work at their own pace and in their own time, preferring asynchronous communication modes.

CALL teacher education processes

Teacher education, as well as introducing prospective teachers to the theories and pedagogies of learning, needs to model the pedagogies it espouses. Earlier, we saw how both Bax (2011) and Motteram (2013b) stated that technology needs to be considered as sociocultural. Bax, basing his arguments on Bijker's (1997) theory of sociotechnical change, proposes that technology in language teaching needs to be considered in a 'social constructivist "contextualist" framework' (p. 4). This positioning of CALL is supported by Motteram et al.'s (2013) claim that general second language teacher education is increasingly taking a sociocultural perspective. They argue that CALL teacher education should follow suit and move away from its more cognitive second language acquisition roots. This alignment is already occurring, as can be seen in the orientation of many of the courses discussed in this volume (e.g., Chapters 2, 7, 8, 9 and 10). I argue that second language teaching itself is increasingly taking such an orientation. Therefore, the processes used in CALL teacher education need to mirror this social constructivist approach to teaching and learning. This speaks to CALL teacher educators designing their courses to use the methodologies Bax (2011) proposes, including interaction, scaffolding, modelling, challenging and reflecting. Many of these are attributes of the courses described in this volume. Students are asked to reflect on their learning and on their technology use, they interact and challenge each other via discussion boards, they collaborate in group activities and assignments, CALL affordances are modelled as they use them for their course, they are challenged to create their own CALL materials, and they move from current knowledge to new. In other words, they learn much of the technology by using it to meet course requirements, such as discussion lists so that they experience communities of practice. As well as facilitating their own learning during CALL teacher education, it creates a model for ongoing professional development. Since Egbert, Paulus, and Nakamichi (2002) found that their teachers largely learned about new CALL activities from their colleagues, CALL teacher education can facilitate ongoing interaction by initiating communities of practice. Aston University's online language teacher education programmes provide such a model. They have a type of discussion list that current students as well as alumni use for interaction, providing 'the participants with an opportunity to be a part of a community, to ask questions, and share thoughts and ideas' (Copland, 2013, p. 4).

Future directions

Missing from the now fairly extensive literature on teacher education in CALL, including the chapters in this volume, is research into the transfer of CALL coursework into the classroom. Some of the authors in this volume have reported on their attempts to address this gap (Chapter 7 by Windeatt; Son, 2014). One of the earliest such research was by Egbert et al. (2002), which found little transfer. Factors other than CALL courses contributed to teachers' use of CALL: previous experience with technology, time constraints, institutional support and learning from colleagues, many of these factors are beyond the control of the teachers themselves. They did not, however, suggest that CALL teacher education should be abandoned, but that '[t]eacher educators need to address the theoretical underpinnings of CALL and present guidelines for effective technology use in context-based situations' (p. 122).

Son (2014) is the most recent study of the uptake of CALL coursework to actual teaching practice. His study, like that of Egbert et al., indicated that teachers often do not use CALL because of their time constraints and other institutional barriers such as poor access to computers or curriculum restrictions. These respondents also agreed with those of Egbert et al., that they found informal means of developing their expertise in CALL: through websites, colleagues and experience. These findings support the multi-teacher collaborative action research study of Murray and McPherson (2005), which demonstrated how transfer of CALL to classroom practice can be enhanced because 'when teachers work together to share experiences and solve specific problems, they expand their knowledge and change their practice' (p. 129). Son also called for the formation of teacher sharing networks. Son further found that language teachers use computers widely, so, it would seem that their reluctance to use CALL with their learners is not based on their own lack of knowledge about computers. Those teachers who do use CALL tasks in their language classrooms found that 'the [CALL] coursework has inspired them to explore innovative ways of using CALL in the classroom' (p. 146).

It would seem, therefore, that for teachers to effectively use CALL in their classrooms requires (a) formal CALL coursework, (b) institutional support and (c) ongoing professional development. The teacher educators reported in this volume have taken up this challenge.

References

Anstey, M., & Bull, G. (2011). Helping teachers to explore multimodal texts. *Curriculum and Leadership Journal*, *8*(16). Retrieved from http://www.curriculum.edu.au/leader/helping_teachers_to_explore_multimodal_texts,31522.html?issueID=12141

Avalos, G. (2015, June 16). Survey: Digital gap persists, *San Jose Mercury News*, pp. B5-6.

Bax, S. (2003). CALL – past, present, and future. *System, 31*(1), 13–28.

Bax, S. (2011). Normalisation revisited: The effective use of technology in language education. *International Journal of Computer-assisted Language Learning and Teaching, 1*(2), 1–15. Retrieved from http://www.academia.edu/3754724/Normalisation_Revisited_The_Effective_Use_of_Teachnology_in_Language_Education

Bijker, W. (1997). *Of bicycles, bakelites, and bulbs: Toward a theory of sociotechnical change*. Cambridge: Cambridge University Press.

Burns, A., & Richards, C. (Eds.). (2009). *The Cambridge guide to second language education*. Cambridge, UK: Cambridge University Press.

Chappelle, C. (2001). *Computer applications in second language acquisition: Foundations for teaching, testing and research*. Cambridge: Cambridge University Press.

Colpaert, J. (2014, May). *Teacher education and integration: Reassuring lies versus inconvenient truths*. Paper presented at the EuroCALL Teacher Education SIG Workshop, Nice, France. https://sites.google.com/site/teacheredsignice/programme/keynotes/teachereducationandictintegrationreassuringliesversusinconvenienttruths

Copland, F. (2013). Distance learning at Aston University. Retrieved from http://www.tirfonline.org/wp-content/uploads/2013/02/TIRF_OLTE_CaseReport2_Copland.pdf

Cornell University Library (2015). Evaluating web pages: Questions to consider, 2015, from http://guides.library.cornell.edu/evaluating_Web_pages

Davies, G., Otto, S. E. K. & Rüschoff, B. (2013). Historical perspectives on CALL. In M. Thomas, H. Reinders & M. Warschauer (Eds.), *Contemporary computer-assisted language learning* (pp. 19–38). London: Bloomsbury.

Debski, R. (2006). *Project-based language teaching with technology*. Sydney: NCELTR.

Dudeney, G., & Hockly, N. (2012). ICT in ELT: How did we get here and where are we going? *ELT Journal, 66*(4), 533–542.

Egbert, J., Paulus, T. M., & Nakamichi, Y. (2002). The impact of CALL instruction on classroom computer use: A foundation for rethinking technology in teacher education. *Language Learning & Technology, 6*(3), 108–126. Retrieved from http://llt.msu.edu/vol6num3/egbert/default.html

Felix, U. (2001). *Beyond Babel: Language learning online*. Melbourne: Language Australia.

Healey, D., Hanson-Smith, E., Hubbard, P., Ioannou-Georgiou, S., Kessler, G., & Ware, P. (2011). *TESOL technology standards: Description, implementation, integration*. Alexandria: Teachers of English to Speakers of other Languages, Inc.

Heift, T., & Schulze, M. (2007). *Errors and intelligence in computer-assisted language learning*. New York: Routledge.

Higgins, J., & Johns, T. (1984). *Computers in language learning*. London: Collins.

Hockly, N. (2013). Designer learning: The teacher as designer of mobile-based classroom learning experiences. Retrieved from http://www.tirfonline.org/english-in-theworkforce/mobile-assisted-language-learning/

Hubbard, P., & Levy, M. (2006a). The scope of CALL education. In P. Hubbard & M. Levy (Eds.), *Teacher education in CALL* (pp. 3–20). Amsterdam: John Benjamins.

Hubbard, P., & Levy, M. (Eds.). (2006b). *Teacher education in CALL*. Amsterdam: John Benjamins.

Internet World Stats. (2015). Internet usage statistics: The internet big picture, from http://www.internetworldstats.com/stats.htm

Kim, D., Rueckert, D., Kim, D.-J., & Seo, S. (2013). Students' perceptions and experiences of mobile learning. *Language Learning & Technology*, *17*(3), 52–73.

Lipscomb, P. (2005). Online without a rope. In Denise Murray & P. McPherson (Eds.), *Navigating to read; reading to navigate* (pp. 99–124). Sydney: NCELTR.

Motteram, G. (2013a). Developing and extending our understanding of language learning and technology. In G. Motteram (Ed.), *Innovations in learning technologies for English language teaching* (pp. 175–192). London: British Council. Retrieved from http://englishagenda.britishcouncil.org/books-resource-packs/innovations-learning-technologies-english-language-teaching

Motteram, G. (2013b). Introduction. In G. Motteram (Ed.), *Innovations in learning technologies for English language teaching* (pp. 5–13). London: British Council. Retrieved from http://englishagenda.britishcouncil.org/sites/ec/files/British%20Council%20Innovations%20in%20Learning%20Technologies%20for%20ELT.pdf

Motteram, G., Slaouti, D., & Onat-Stelma, Z. (2013). Second language teacher education in CALL: An alignment of practice and theory. In J. Thomas, H. Reinders, & M. Warchauer (Eds.), *Contemporary computer-assisted language learning* (pp. 55–71). London: Bloomsbury.

Murray, D. E. (1999). Access to information technology: Considerations for language educators. *Prospect*, *14*(3), 4–12.

Murray, D. E. (2005). New frontiers in technology and teaching. In C. Davison (Ed.), *Information technology and innovation in language education* (pp. 25–44). Hong Kong: University of Hong Kong Press.

Murray, D. E., & McPherson, P. (Eds.). (2005). *Navigating to read; reading to navigate*. Sydney: NCELTR.

Murray, D. E. (2013). Technology and literacy. In C. A. Chappelle (Ed.), *The encyclopedia of applied linguistics*. Oxford, UK: Wiley-Blackwell.

Murray, D. E., & Christison, M. A. (2017). Going online: Affordances and limitations for teachers and teacher educators. In K. Hyland & L. Wong (Eds.), *Faces of English education: Students, teachers and pedagogy*. London: Continuum.

Nielsen, J. (2003). Homepage real estate allocation. Retrieved from http://www.useit.com/alertbox/20030210.html

Pegrum, M. (2014). *Mobile learning: Languages, literacies, and cultures*. London: Palgrave Macmillan.

Peters, M. (2006). Developing computer competencies for pre-service language teachers. In P. Hubbard & M. Levy (Eds.), *Teacher education in CALL* (pp. 153–165). Amsterdam: John Benjamins.

Prensky, M. (2001). Digital natives, digital immigrants. *On the Horizon*, *9*(5). Retrieved from http://dx.doi.org/10.1108/10748120110424816

Puentedura, R. (2011). A brief introduction to TPCK and SAMR. Freeport workshop slides, 8 December, from http://hippasus.com/rrpweblog/archives/2011/12/08/BriefIntroTPCKSAMR.pdf

Reinders, H., & White, C. (2011). Learner autonomy and new learning environments. *Language Learning and Technology*, *15*(3), 1–3.

Richards, J. C., & Nunan, D. (Eds.) (1990). *Second language teacher education*. Cambridge, UK: Cambridge University Press.

Schwienhorst, K. (2004). Native-speaker/non-native-speaker discourse in the MOO: Topic negotiation and initiation in a synchronous text-based environment. *Computer Assisted Language Learning*, *17*(1), 35–50.

Son, J.-B. (2014). Moving beyond basics: From CALL coursework to classroom practice and professional development. In J.-B. Son (Ed.), *Computer-assisted language learning: Learners, teachers and tools* (pp. 122–149). Newcastle upon Tyne, UK: Cambridge Scholars Publishing.

Tindale, J. (2005). Reading print and electronic texts. In D. E. Murray & P. McPherson (Eds.), *Navigating to read; reading to navigate*. Sydney, Australia: NCELTR.

Tomlinson, B. (2011). *Materials development in language teaching*. Cambridge, UK: Cambridge University Press.

Warchauer, M. (1996). Computer-assisted language learning: An introduction. In S. Fotos (Ed.), *Multimedia language teaching* (pp. 3–20). Tokyo: Logos International.

Warschauer, M. (2000). The changing global economy and the future of English teaching. *TESOL Quarterly*, *34*(3), 511–535.

Index

CPSIA information can be obtained
at www.ICGtesting.com
Printed in the USA
LVHW03*1957111018
593276LV00010B/183/P

9 781350 020405